"Lisa Copen's care for those around her with invisible illnesses is a role model for churches worldwide. With one in every two people dealing with pain, Lisa's practical wisdom sheds much needed light on the silent majority sitting in our pews and helps us reach out with the compassion of Christ."
Pam Farrel, author of over 30 books including best-selling "Men are Like Waffles, Women are Like Spaghetti"

How to Start a Chronic Illness Small Group Ministry

Discovering your passion
Defining your purpose
Debuting your program

LISA J. COPEN

Rest Ministries Publishers
SAN DIEGO, CA

Table of Contents

Special Thanks

When I wrote my first book on beginning a chronic illness ministry in one's church in 1997, it was based on research, a little bit of experience, and feedback from people who shared their stories. Now, years later I graciously am able to thank each person who has called, emailed, posted something online, or chatted with me about his or her experience in leading a small group ministry. Your knowledge as leaders have shaped this book, and it is my hope that the reader will find delight is seeing her own concerns or experiences spelled out on paper and know she is not alone.

A very special thank you goes to Carol Bock who proofed the book on a very short deadline to help me get it finished within my timeline.

And I could not have done this without the support of my husband, Joel, who helped me with daily tasks and as always, encourages me with my dreams. Thank you to my 7-year-old son, Joshua, for all the times I said, "Just a minute. . . Mommy needs to finish this sentence" and he actually waited patiently. I worked on this book while watching my son's karate class, at amusement parks while he and his dad went on roller coasters, to many medical waiting rooms.

Most of all, I thank my precious Lord and Savoir for giving me the opportunity to do what I love—to write . . . especially for Him. Despite joint replacement surgery weeks before I began this book, it's the fastest book I have written and it's due to God's provision of a computer voice program and new silicone joints in my hand. Every time I thought it would never get done, God gave me just enough energy to get to the next step. I pray that I have honored Him by providing tools toward the creation of new ministries for those who are hurting for His glory.

*"Be kind, for everyone you meet
is fighting a hard battle."*
Plato

*"Out of our own experiences and knowledge
of the Trinity's consolations, we realize how much we
have to give to others who are enduring adversities.
We discern what suits us and might be a solace to them.
We are also more alert to those who are suffering
but trying to hide it, and thereby we can both
assist them and encourage them to let their
needs be known to the community of support."*
Marva J. Dawn, Being Well When We're Ill:
Wholeness and Hope in Spite of Infirmity

*"God does not want our ability,
but our availability." Anonymous*

*"The Lord has a purpose for each of our lives.
Disability doesn't change that.
Tragedy doesn't erase His plans for us.
He created us with special and
unique gifts and talents."*
Zanina Jacinto, And He Will Lift You Up

Introduction

Consider your insights and *inspiration* (passions). The gifts God has given you to discern and fulfill your call also include the *passions* you've developed over the course of your education, your work and life experience, and God's other dealings with you along the way. You may have a burning insight or feel a nagging inspiration about a particular concern. *Why doesn't anybody do something about that problem?* you wonder. *It seems so obvious to me that something could be done in this area*, you think. *Somebody really ought to. . .* you muse.

When we finally say yes to this call, it may be costly. Like Jesus, "who for the joy set before him endured the cross" (Hebrews 12:2), however, a Christian leader feels a fire in the belly that can't be put out even in adversity rains down. Like Jesus, who told the disciples when they were concerned that He'd skipped a meal, "My food is to do the will of Him who sent me and to finish His work" (John 4:34) a leader will often feel nourished by fixing a problem or seizing a ministry opportunity.[1]

You may be a pastor or other church leadership member, but the majority of people who are reading this book are in fact chronically ill. So let me take a moment just to acknowledge that your journey thus far should be celebrated. Getting out of bed each morning despite significant physical pain is an accomplishment in itself. Diving into ministry with people who are also hurting takes a special gift.

A broken body can have a great deal of power over our spirit if we allow it. Charles Kingsley once said, "Pain is no evil, unless it conquers us." If you are reading this book, I rejoice alongside you that your pain has not conquered you. It may even feel as if God has allowed this illness into your life and has said, "This is your mission. Now you can choose *how* you wish to accept it." Author and disability advocate Joni Eareckson Tada says, "When we suffer and handle it with grace, we're like walking billboards advertising the positive way God works in the life of someone who suffers."[2] Author Phillip Yancey explains that pain can also define us in a way that is not healthy: "Pain narrows vision. The most private of sensations, it forces us to think of ourselves and little else."[3]

Every day I gain a deeper respect for those who live with chronic illness as well as those in ministry. Living with a chronic illness is not easy. Being a leader also has its share of challenges. Both can leave you wanting to throw your hands up in the air and sigh, "I surrender, Lord. I just surrender!"

The fact that God has created a stirring in your heart to combine these two challenges — living with illness and leading a small group ministry — reveal to me that you are an incredibly special person. I am honored that you hold this book in your hand and I hope that you will connect with me and other leaders of small group ministries on our web site[1] to share your questions, concerns and praises.

You may have picked up this book for a variety of reasons. Perhaps:

---

[1] The web site is at RestMinistries.com or the social network is at RestMinistriesSunroom.com

- ☙ You have a chronic illness
- Someone you love has a chronic illness
- You want to start a small group/support group at your church
- You want to teach your church awareness regarding illness
- You're just curious where disability issues and religion merge

Joy and wisdom is ours through every lesson or experience as we grow closer to Christ and fulfill the plan that He has for our lives.

And doing it with a lack of perfect health is an incredible way to honor God. Even Satan believes that the health, or rather, the un-health, of our bodies is one of the most practical and effective ways to exasperate our spirit.

In the book of Job, Job responds favorably to God, despite all of the suffering that God has allowed to befall him—the loss of his livestock, home, and his family. But Satan is sure that by attacking Job's body he will finally win by seeing Job curse God.

"Skin for skin!" Satan tells God. "A man will give all he has for his own life. But stretch out Your hand and strike his flesh and bones, and he will surely curse You to Your face." (Job 2:4) And although Job was faithful to God, he and God "had it out." Job also had some harsh words, depressing thoughts, doubts, and questions about what God was doing.

> "Why is life given to a man whose way is hidden, whom God has hedged in?. . . What I feared has come upon me; what I dreaded has happened to me. I have no peace, no quietness; I have no rest, but only turmoil." (Job 3:23, 25, 26)

Have you been there? Remember that even Job lost everything he held dear and had invested his life into. But still he stuck with God, trusting God completely. . . and then he started seeing those boils appear on his skin. Between his lesions, his wife's nagging, and his friend's well intentioned but not helpful remarks, he'd had enough! And he decided to tell God about it. But if you've read the end of the story you know that in the end it all worked out.

> "Then Job replied to the Lord: 'I know that you can do all things; no plan of yours can be thwarted' . . . After Job had prayed for his friends, the Lord made him prosperous again and gave him twice as much as he had before. The Lord blessed the latter part of Job's life more than the first. After this, Job lived a hundred and forty years; he saw his children and their children to the fourth generation. And so he died, old and full of years."[4]

I share this with you to remind you that you are human just like Job. There will be times you want to throw in the towel as well as times you see God bless you in ways you never asked or imagined. You may have friends give well-meaning advice, yet it totally misses the mark of where you are at spiritually. And the most unlikely acquaintance may simply give you a hug and shed a tear with you.

The importance of prayer

As we move forward through this book discovering the possibilities of small group ministry to the chronically ill, remember to give yourself the same grace that God gives to you. When you are feeling overwhelmed, ask yourself this simple question: "Am I now trying to win the approval of men, or of God? Or am I trying to please men? As Galatians

1:10 tells us, "If I were still trying to please men, I would not be a servant of Christ."

If you are feeling at wits end, it's likely that you are trying to please men, because God won't ever ask you to do something without giving you the tools to do it. And sometimes the "men" we are trying to please are actually ourselves. Our own expectations can be our worst downfall.

But the most important thing I want to stress at the beginning of this book, however, is that despite your ability to follow through with each step and organize in the most efficient manner, it all will be fruitless without prayer and a daily walk with God. A study was done by smallgroups.com and here are their findings regarding prayer.

> "Eighty-three percent of leaders with a strong prayer life reported that at least one person had come to Jesus through the influence of their group, whereas only 19 percent of leaders with a weak prayer life could say the same. It didn't surprise us that leaders with a growing relationship with God had groups that were bringing more people to Christ, but it was shocking how much of a difference it makes. Leaders with a strong prayer life have groups that, on average, have more than four times the evangelistic impact as groups led by leaders with a weak prayer life."[5]

John 15:5 says, "I am the vine; you are the branches. If a man remains in Me and I in him, he will bear much fruit; apart from Me you can do nothing." Regardless of what tips you may discover in this book, remember to keep prayer always the first priority. John 15:5 *doesn't* say, "I am the vine, you are the branches and he who has the most resources, books, mentorship, funds, time and energy will bear much fruit." With the gift of prayer, God has equipped you with the most precious and essential tool to do the work that He has prepared in advance for you to do (Ephesians 2:10).

Together we can create a small group for those who live with chronic illness--one that is not just a typical secular setting where people sit around and compare notes on the horrors of chronic illnesses, but rather an oasis where people can feel safe and comfortable in sharing the daily challenges of their condition and what gets them through it.

> "Praise God! I thank the Lord for starting another group. When I think about how much I've been helped by HopeKeepers®[2]. and how it kept me from suicide by helping to answer all those tough questions I had inside concerning my suffering . . .I am just so thankful to Him for sending us out to start new groups to help others find Him in their pain. Keep up His work and if you have a group night where no one shows up, just spend the time in prayer for the others." -Matt

In my years of ministry with the chronically ill, I've heard from many people who are overflowing with zeal about this calling they feel that God has given to them; they feel a passion to not only create a place where lives can dramatically be changed but where people can discover true hope and fellowship that can only come through Jesus Christ.

I understand this calling, because God placed it on my heart in 1995 and Rest Ministries is the result of my response to that call. Even when I am at my weakest physically or spiritually, I still know that this fervor for chronic illness ministry is something the Lord has instilled in my heart and

---

[2] Throughout this book you will see the name HopeKeepers® used frequently and sometimes interchangeably with "illness small group" or "illness support group." HopeKeepers is the small group program of Rest Ministries, Inc.

that the flame will only burn out if God chooses to pull out His snuffer.

People who have a chronic illness suffer in a new and different way then they may have ever experienced before their daily dose of pain. This is one of the reasons I believe that those who have a chronic illness feel like they are in an accelerated learning program when it comes to suffering and the process and power of God's refinement.

So where do you start? I don't think I could say it better than Winny who leads a chronic illness small group:

> "Here are some of the non-tangible things to do. Pray, pray, pray! Pray that God give you the wisdom, discernment and compassion to lead this group. Praise God that you already have the heart and obedience. Rebuke the devil because he will put fear and insecurity into your heart and mind. Pray that God will send those who need this help and support to your meetings. Pray that you and your church leadership will be of one accord in this undertaking. And mostly pray that the Holy Spirit will be present at the meetings because it is He who does the healing. I'm not speaking of physical healing—although we pray for that too, if it is God's will. The healing I'm talking about is the peace, comfort and wholeness that only God can give as you *live with* a chronic illness." -Winny

*"Befriend your loneliness, pick up your cross . . .
Precisely where we are painful, precisely where we are
suffering there is the gateway that leads us to something
new...if we are willing to embrace our brokenness we will
discover that in the midst of all this pain there is joy."*
Henri Nouwen

*"The ultimate measure of a man is not where
he stands in moments of comfort, but where he
stands at times of challenge and controversy."*
Martin Luther King, Jr.

"He jests at scars who never felt a wound."
Shakespeare

*"If there were no suffering, would there be
compassion? If there were no discipline and hardship,
would we ever learn patience and endurance? Construct
a universe with no trouble in it and immediately you
banish some of the finest qualities in the world."*
James Stewart

*"Comfort and prosperity have never
enriched the world as much as adversity has."*
Billy Graham

*"It is in the quiet crucible of your personal
private sufferings that your noblest dreams
are born and God's greatest gifts are given in
compensation for what you've been through"*
Wintley Phipp

CHAPTER 1

Understanding chronic illness

"My 9-year-old son and I were in the grocery store when we ran into a woman from our church that stopped me and said, 'Your mother told me you've been having some bad back problems.' I acknowledged that I had. 'Well,' she replied, 'you don't look like you have any problems!' We finished chatting and she left. My son turned to me and said, 'Mommy, how are you supposed to look with your pain?' He had grown up with my dealing with pain almost all of his young life and I didn't let it interfere in my raising him, but he had a pondering question there that I've never forgotten." — Ellie

There is no doubt that physical pain hurts. The simple fact is that by just being human we are nearly guaranteed that we will experience bodily discomfort at some point in our life, because our bodies are imperfect. Most people undergo an acute physical crisis once or twice a decade, facing the unpleasantness of surgeries and accidents that result in casts and crutches, followed by an eventual recovery.

Chronic pain and chronic illness, however, are never-ending, and it puts those of who live with it in a unique social situation, since we rarely look ill.

If you are reading this book, you likely are eager to find out more about chronic illness and pain ministry. But before we dive into the deep waters, let's take a look at some of the basics such as the question the youngster so easily expressed earlier. *What exactly does chronic illness look like?*

What is a chronic illness?

According to the United States National Center for Health Statistics a chronic illness is an illness "lasting 3 months or more." The term "chronic" comes from the Greek word chronos, which stands for time and means lasting a long time. Occasionally I receive emails from people explaining that they have been suffering from an intense daily condition such as migraines and they ask, "Do I qualify to be a part of your ministry family?"

My answer is always "Yes. If you have to ask, you qualify! Welcome!" When you are the one going through the pain, you may be counting time according to hours and not weeks or months. Three months can feel like a lifetime when everything in that life starts to topple.

What is the difference between an invisible illness and a visible illness?

"Invisible Chronic Illness" or ICI, was a phrase coined, according to Paul J. Donoghe, in the early nineties when he and Mary Elizabeth Siegel wrote the first edition of the groundbreaking book *Sick and Tired of Feeling Sick and Tired: Living with Invisible Chronic Illness*, (1994). [1]

The invisibility of chronic illness makes it problematic to fully grasp the reality about how many people do not feel nearly as good as they may appear. In fact, you may be surprised to know that nearly 1 in 2 Americans, about 133 million people, live with some kind of illness or chronic condition, such as back pain.[2] That number is projected to increase by more than one percent per year by 2030, resulting in an estimated chronically ill population of 171 million. And, despite popular belief, 60 percent of the chronically ill are between the ages of 18 and 64.[3]

When I began National Invisible Chronic Illness Awareness Week back in 2002, the only statistic I could find about how many people lived with chronic illness or pain was 133 million, but I was not able to wrap by brain around what this looked like. I didn't want a statistic about how many thousands of football field stadiums this was. So I looked up the population of the United States and did a simple math equation. It was about 1 in 3 people. I began to plaster that statistic all over our web site and brochures and soon saw it popping up on the backs of author's book covers, and on web sites in press releases.

With population growth and the increase of illness since 2002 that number is now closer to 1 in 2, so for the past few years you will note our resources say, "Nearly 1 in 2 people live with a chronic condition." I have used this figure in most of our materials for our invisible illness week outreach in order to bring an emotional perspective to both the healthy and the ill about just how prevalent — and invisible — illness is.

I believe one of the first steps in creating awareness about why there should be more small group illness ministries, Christian resources, and congregational care style ministries for the ill, is to help leaders in our churches and communities today understand that those who live with chronic illness are not a small minority or niche population.

We are the people that stand beside you at the grocery store who seem impatient with the long line (because we cannot stand much longer). We are the ones who park in handicapped spots that you stare at, wondering if we are using a privilege that was meant to be for our grandparent.

Creating a greater sense of awareness about how many people actually live with chronic illness that impacts either their own life, or the life of their family, will eventually result in an increase of resources to gain hope and encouragement.

Does this invisible/visible difference really matter?

In planning for an illness ministry, whether an illness is visible or invisible does not make a difference in the way that one is more valid than the other. If one is in pain, she is *in pain*, and her pain should not be compared to anyone else's pain in order for her to feel it is acknowledged and validated.

I have found that it does not matter so much what specific illness one has, his or her experience will still be unique from other people who have that same illness. On the other hand, people will find that they have a great deal in common with others who live with any illness. The emotions and spiritual struggles overlap beyond any diagnosis. Your group may consist of people with a large variety of diseases, but there will be much common ground.

You may also want to consider opening it up to those with cancer, or sharing your resources with the leader of a group for those with cancer. Although cancer can be seen as more of an acute medical condition, there are many side effects that can last the rest of one's life, and the threat of having the cancer return is always present.

As someone who has lived with rheumatoid arthritis since 1993, for most of those years, I have had an invisible illness. Now, after hand deformities, limping from my feet breaking down, and a swollen, puffy face from prednisone, among other visual symptoms, my disease is more visible than it was in the first years of onset. However, my disease is

21

really just more obvious to those who have a chronic illness themselves and know the symptoms of disease and side effects of medications.

To most of the world I am still someone who appears to be healthy because I have no extreme visual symptoms that unequivocally express the magnitude of pain I am in. I don't use a cane or other assistive device, on a daily basis. I don't look "unwell."

How many people have invisible illnesses or disabilities?

Most people believe that the chronically ill live with many seasons of remission and some seasons of pain or post-surgery recovery. The majority of ill people, however, live in seasons of pain where they are trying to function as normally as possible and seasons when life is temporarily on hold as they recover from a severe flare, an infection, illness exasperations or post-surgery recovery.

The majority of us with chronic illness, however, would not describe illness as just a slice of our life, but rather the pie crust upon which every decision we make is impacted. For example, I can be eating dinner at a restaurant at 6 p.m. and feel my neck starting to freeze into place. If I get home by 7 p.m. and take some medication, I still may be awake and in significant pain for 24-48 hours and then be barely able to sit up or walk around for the next 48 hours after that. Flares can come without any warning at any time and last for an indefinite time period.

According to the statistics, about 96% of people who live with an illness or disability have symptoms that are invisible. Out of 26 million persons who are considered to have a severe disability, only 7 million use a visible device for mobility. Thus, 19 million of the people who were defined as severely disabled, do not use a wheelchair, cane, crutches, or walkers. In other words, 73% of Americans with severe disabilities do not use such devices. Therefore, a disability cannot be determined solely on whether or not a person uses visible assistive equipment.[4]

It should be pointed out that those who have visible conditions also have their own share of troubles and many would love to trade in their wheelchair for those uncomfortable stares those with invisible illness may receive when they legally park in the blue handicapped parking place. Typically, people who use assistive devices are considered "disabled" rather than just "chronically ill", but many diseases go from one state to another. For example, diseases such as multiple sclerosis or dystonia can be an illness when first diagnosed, but as symptoms become more severe it becomes a disabling disease.

The most important thing for you to note, as one who is interested in beginning a chronic illness/pain ministry is that these differences in appearance *do* make a large difference in how a person may or may not feel his illness is understood and his experiences validated. Chronic illness is usually thought to be a physical condition, but for many people, as they go through that grief cycle over and over with each new loss of abilities, they may experience more difficulty in coping with the social and emotional aspects of the illness than the actual physical pain.

As you read through this book and make your plans for the ministry you are considering, keep in mind the different people your small group ministry could serve. For example:
- men and women, adults and teenagers
- those who have just been diagnosed and those who have lived with an illness for decades
- seniors who live at home independently and seniors in assisted living

- people who are single and people who have families at home
- parents of very young children and parents of adult children
- people who have hired caregivers and people who have volunteer caregivers, such as a family member
- those who are bedridden a good portion of the time and those who work full-time
- those who are finacially blessed and those who are trying to survive on disability assistance
- those who are ill, but who are also a caregiver for someone such as for an aging parent or an autistic child

You may encounter a woman who has had multiple sclerosis for twenty years, but who is just now beginning to use a wheelchair and grieving the loss of her mobility and the frustration of feeling like people don't treat her the same.

You may find yourself ministering to a man who is in his twenties who looks perfectly healthy and who competed in your community marathon last year, but who has now been diagnosed with fibromyalgia (FM or FMS). Perhaps he is going through the emotions of not being able to do what he once did and being told he over did his training last year — and so it's his fault he is now ill. He may even be teased that fibromyalgia is that "woman's disease."

You may find yourself talking with a new mother who was recently dianosed with diabetes, and despite the fact that she looks fine and has a healthy baby, she is now struggling to take care of her new child while learning about all the demands of this illness and wondering if she will survive the toddler years.

You will not have to address each situation individually in your group setting during your lesson plans, but it's important to remember that those who have illnesses are just like the rest of the population. Situation vary, lifestyles differ, and life happens.

Though illness often demands to be the number one priority in our lives, it does not always over-rule all other situations. Children are married, grandkids are born, spouses get cancer, and there are many moments of laughter through tears.

Larry Crabb shares in his book *Inside Out*, "The richest love grows in the soil of an unbearable disappointment with life. When we realize life can't give us what we want, we can better give up our foolish demand that it do so and get on with the noble task of loving, as we should. We will no longer need to demand protection from further disappointment. The deepest change will occur in the life of a bold realist who clings to God with a passion only his realistic appraisal of life can generate."[5]

*"The way to love someone is to lightly
run your finger over that person's soul
until you find a crack and then gently
pour your love into that crack."*
Keith Miller

*"Thank God we're not calling the shots. He is. And
although there are aspects of 'winning' that are good,
God builds churches a different way. Jesus says, 'Go out
into the streets and alleys... find [the weak]... make them
come in... so that my Father's house maybe full' (Luke
14). God wants His house filled with inadequate and
weak people. That way, everyone focuses on the strength
of the Lord rather than the skill and wisdom of man."*
Joni Eareckson Tada, Pearls of Great Price

*"To the weak I became weak, to win the weak. I have
become all things to all men so that by all possible
means I might save some. "1 Corinthians 9:22*

*"If I had my choice in selecting teachers
for any activity of a local church, I would not
first seek those who have the greatest academic
credentials. I would seek a person who is open and
responsive, who loves Jesus Christ, and who is growing."*
Larry Richards, The Reason for our Hope Foundation

CHAPTER 2

How will a chronic illness small group help?

> "HopeKeepers to me is understanding, support of others, plus learning to understand the pain I live with through Jesus' eyes; which enables me, in turn, to help others to know Jesus and understand His love for them. HopeKeepers has certainly caused me to rethink and cope more successfully."-Shelley

Look at these statistics and tell me if it is time for the church to step in and take a second look at why a small group chronic illness ministry may be beneficial.

The divorce rate among the chronically ill is over 75 percent[1] and depression is 15-20% higher for the chronically ill than for the average person[2]. Various studies have reported that physical illness or uncontrollable physical pain are major factors in up to 70% of suicides[3] and more than 50% of these suicidal patients were under 35 years of age.[4]

So, what is the good news? There is a lot! Here are just a few of the findings about the influence faith has on our health or illness:

- The significance of one's faith has shown to lower one's risk of depressive symptoms and aid one in better handling a stressful medical event.[5]
- Teenagers who have some level of "spirituality" cope better with the condition of chronic illness than those

who do not. Researchers also found that one of the most important predictors of poorer overall quality of life was having a poorer sense of spiritual well-being.[6]

- A survey of more than a thousand practicing physicians found that 56% believe religion and spirituality have a significant effect on their patient's health. 76% of the physicians believed that spirituality helps patients cope, 74% said that it gives patients a positive state of mind, while 55% reported that spirituality and religion provide emotional and practical support via the religious community.[7]

- Those who use their religious faith to cope are significantly less depressed, even when taking into account the severity of their physical illness. In fact, the clinical effects of religious coping showed the strongest benefit among those with severe physical disability. Some 87 patients hospitalized with serious illness who also then suffered depression were followed over time in another study. The patients with a deep, internalized faith recovered faster from the depression, even when their physical condition *wasn't* improving.[8]

So we know that (1) nearly 1 in 2 people have a chronic illness; (2) a good portion of them are desperately hurting; and (3) having a faith to depend on makes a significant difference in their lives—so much so that it actually can influence their physical symptoms or how well they cope with their illness. Could we find a more hurting yet receptive group of people to minister to?

Even those who claim they don't believe in God, are staring up at the stars demanding answers.

- Where is God?

- Is there a God?
- How am I going to make it through this?
- Why is God allowing me to be ill when I've tried to be a good person?
- What am I going to do with my life if I can fulfill the plans I had or am unable to work?
- How will I be able to take care of my family or not become a burden to them?

They may reach out to their friends for answers, or, if they have any kind of home church, they may turn to it for clarification and comfort.

But how does our church typically respond? Best-selling author Philip Yancey writes in *Where is God When it Hurts?* "The problem of pain. . . is a problem of relationship. Many people want to love God, but cannot see past their tears. They feel hurt and betrayed. Sadly, the church often responds with more confusion than comfort."[9]

When a person is ill, the church's response is often to pray for the healing of the person. But when the person is not healed the church leaders quietly turn away out of frustration and bewilderment. If God chooses not to heal, what more can be done? Isn't it up to the ill person to figure out what may be preventing his healing and then get back to them when he is ready to try again?

Do individuals in a church represent the whole church?

Like the rest of the world, the church[3] body is imperfect because it is made up of people, all of us who are sinners.

---

[3] The term "church" is used in this book as a broad, all-inclusive designation of any religious body, denomination, etc. in the broadest sense.

And when it comes to acknowledging physical pain and chronic illness, unfortunately, the church seems swept up with the rest of society. Unknowingly, the church can become blind to this hurting group of people and uninformed about ways in which to minister to them. It may be just one or two people within the church body that says something ignorant. But in a time of deep pain, when a person hears a response that is less than kind or not very sympathetic, she may believe that this individual represents the whole church's beliefs about illness. Let's look at Cathy's experience.

> "I seriously considered what I could do for vacation Bible school, and decided that I should just try to make snacks. A lady who was my age was watching me sign up on the snack sheet, and she chided me, telling me that snacks was what the [elderly] ladies sign up for and that I should be signing up to help with the kids. I know she didn't understand that I have to conserve energy for work, housework, and my family, so I just laughed and signed on the snack sheet. A few months ago when I was still on the steroids, I might have broken down and cried. It's painful to think about how I once was able to do a lot more. Being new at church, where no one knows that, makes it worse." — Cathy

These kind of experiences make me sad because when people are in pain they are oftentimes searching and open to comfort — possibly even receptive to God's love even if they have had a hardened heart in the past. They have questions and are searching for life tools to get them through this time when everything else they have tried is failing. Oscar Wilde once said, "How else but through a broken heart may Lord Christ enter in?" Let us not miss this opportunity to share about Jesus when people's once hardened hearts are breaking.

What makes churches receptive to starting chronic illness small group ministries?

By reading the stories from people who live with illness or pain, you will come to see the need for change in our churches. You will more fully understand the great need for support from our friends, our peers in Christ.

When I first began Rest Ministries in 1996 many people said that they would love to have a small group in their church where they could talk about what they were experiencing on this bumpy road of chronic illness. The result was an international program of Rest Ministries, Inc., a small group ministry for those with illness or pain called HopeKeepers®. HopeKeepers is a place where a person can feel safe. It's a sanctuary; a place where people can pour out their souls regarding everything in their life, but especially about the physical ailments and their relationship with Christ.

Naturally, after kicking off my own HopeKeepers group, I decided to approach churches within my community. I explained that there were likely people who were sitting in their church pews who lived with chronic illness or pain who would find a small group/Bible study environment helpful in order to cope with the challenges of chronic illness. I attempted to describe just how significantly illness can impact individual lives as well as the lives of the person's family.

In time, what I discovered was that I was going about this the wrong way. Although I could create a fancy brochure that conveyed the need for a small group for those with chronic illness, there was no telling who's hands it would fall into once it was delivered to the church. And although a church secretary may find it interesting, and even pass it on to a pastor, the likelihood that someone would actually call me to find out more about Rest Ministries and how to start an illness ministry in the church was extremely slim.

I quickly understood that the best way to stir up an interest in the church itself, was for me to sit back and wait for people to come forard who were already in a particular church who felt God's calling to lead such a group. Then these people would take the idea to their church leadership to see if a HopeKeepers group may be a possibility, with the intent to lead the group if the church said yes. This is typically how churches begin illness small group ministries today. A large part of the reason is that the majority of churches prefer not to begin a new ministry without appointing someone in advance who will take on its responsibilities.

Understanding why churches are apprehensive

Just because one attends a church does not mean the church will immediately be receptive to the idea. Church members who express an interest in leading a HopeKeepers group must have an idea about what makes their church tick. How can a person make it easy for the church to say "yes"? By understanding why and when the leadership in the church has said "yes" to other ministries or programs.

For example, when my husband and I moved to a new church in the year 2000, I heard from people involved in our church say that the church's overall style of adopting new church programs was to bypass parachurch ministry programs[4] that already existed, such as Promise Keepers,

---

[4] According to Wikapedia, "Parachurch organizations are Christian faith-based organizations which carry out their mission usually independent of church oversight. The prefix para, is Greek for beside, or alongside."

Moms in Touch, or MOPS (Mothers of Preschoolers). Instead, they frequently took the bare-bones of ministries that already existed and then adapted them to fit their own needs.

I understood that if I went into the church with a "glorious plan" to create a chronic illness ministry it would be met with some predictable skepticism and I would likely miss my opportunity. So I sat back and waited for a few *years* to allow God to work it out in His own timing. This was extremely difficult for me. I am one who rarely waits for God to open a door, but rather one who gets out my crow bar and hollers, "Lord, I'm comin' through! Stop me if you don't want me here!" But I practised patience and humbly realized that I should not assume anything. I waited to see if God even wanted my ministry to be represented in my own church. And He did.

One of the pastors of my church expressed to his neighbor how multitudes of people were coming in for counseling who had a chronic illness, and he wondered what was availalbe that could help the church improve how they served those with illness. His neighbor, "happened to be" on Rest Ministries Board of Directors and when he told the pastor about Rest Ministries and our HopeKeepers small group program, the pastor asked "How can I get in touch with this Lisa Copen?" He responded, "Actually, she goes to your church."

Within a week I received a phone call, met with the pastor and discussed Rest Ministries. Within about six months I was invited to speak on chronic illness at the church, and within a year we had a HopeKeepers group that has now been active for over five years.

I can say without a doubt, that had I gone to my church's leadership team when I first began attending church, "spread

out my wares," and told them how my ministry could begin
to address some of the needs of the church—
especially those that they were not even aware of—I would
have been gently turned away. Not only would I be
promoting a parachurch ministry program that the church
customarily steers away from, but I would also lack
humbleness. It's important for us to remember that we must
actually attend a church for a while before we go in and try to
change things.

I share this story with you so that you can understand
that despite the fact Rest Ministries is one of the few, and one
of the largest Christian organizations that specifically serves
those who live a chronic illness, in my own church and my
community, I am just an average person who happens to live
with rheumatoid arthritis.

When I approach churches about how they can improve
their chronic illness or pain ministry outreach, I sometimes
still encouter skepticism and uncertainty. For years Rest
Ministries has been an afiliate ministry of Joni and Friends
International Disability Center and this has increased pastors'
assurance in the ministry and its theology, and yet my
motives and goals are occasionally questioned. And frankly,
most churches believe they already have "illness ministry"
covered. They have a few women who deliver casseroles and
cookies when people have surgery and so far, that seems to
be working out just fine. Why change it and make it more
complicated?

We fear for our own vulnerabilities

There is another reason many people like to shuffle those
with problems out the back door: it doesn't sit well with us
that life has moments when it is just not fair or explainable.
There is no shortage of people who are eager to point out that
there must be *something* that an ill person has done, not done,

said, not confessed, etc. that has caused his suffering. It reminds me of the childhood reminder "When you point a finger at someone there are three fingers pointing back at you."

The truth is that none of us like to be reminded of our vulnerability and so it is easier for us to believe that the person who has an illness or disability must have it for a reason that is logical and just. God is a loving God who is all-powerful, so He would not allow this person to suffer unless there was a reason, right?

> "I have used a wheelchair for eighteen years. What does it mean to the average person to encounter me? Whatever else it may mean, it is to be reminded of his/her own vulnerability and the vulnerability of those whom they love. To be reminded, at however deep a level, that they and theirs are but a traffic accident, a fall, a dive into a too-shallow pool away from being — in their language—a cripple, or. worse yet, a 'helpless cripple.' To be reminded that even in their sleep in the safety of their homes, a sinister disease can creep in and begin chewing away at nerve and muscle tissue, undetected until it is too late. They see me as loss, as option no longer available, as life's hopes and dreams aborted. Life as existing, not flourishing. And ultimately, as a harbinger of their own final vulnerability, death".[10]

We can most easily accept suffering if we understand the reason. But what if there seems to be no logical explanation for it? Well then, in order to avoid forcing ourselves to accept that we too are vulnerable, we can quietly reassure ourselves, "Perhaps that person has unconfessed sin in her life, and that is why she is suffering."

Ironically, the people who I have heard actually say this are under the illusion that they have jumped through all of the confessional hoops God has set up so that there is no possible sliver of unconfessed sin in their own life.

But "all have sinned and fall short of the glory of God" (Romans 3:23). If we acknowledged that there is not always a reasonable or consistent visual purpose for suffering than we may have to face our fear that God could require us to suffer too.

These fears aren't all that unusual. Even Job's friends felt this way when they saw the destruction that God was allowing into Job's life. They knew that Job had been a faithful servant to God, and yet they saw his life being devastated. So what was their response? They condemned Job and told him it was his own fault and that he should just repent so he could get on with life.

Job's friend, Eliphaz, said, "Consider now: Who, being innocent, has ever perished? Where were the upright ever destroyed? As I have observed, those who plow evil and those who sow trouble, reap it. We have examined this, and it is true. So hear it and apply it to yourself," (Job 4:7-8;26,27).

Regardless of the array of emotions we feel, one thing is certain: It's very common to feel awkward fellowshipping with an ill person. She may remind us of our own defenselessness in this imperfect world. She may remind us of our own sin. Seeing her suffer makes us question the wisdom of the God, in whom we put our faith. Would He allow such circumstances to befall us or the ones we love?

In light of this, does the church organize an encouragement ministry for these people who live with pain and need support from one another? So far, the answer has been not likely. We are hoping that this is about to change, because, as a wise man once said, "We should seize every opportunity to give encouragement. It is oxygen to the soul."[11]

What to expect from this book

Whether you are considering starting a chronic illness small group ministry in your church or community, or you are simply brainstorming ideas to see what God may do with this experience of illness you have, know that I have stood in your shoes. I have experienced the same thrill of possibility, as well as the feeling that I am in way over my head. I have felt like every minute of a small group meeting was God ordained and orchestrated. I've also sat alone and cried when I put forth so much effort and energy and no one showed up. I have felt so much excitement over what I could see God doing, and a few days later wondered if I heard God's voice at all or it I was just caught up in something that made me feel good and valued.

I have talked with many people who work for organizations that wish to increase disability outreach in churches today. These people have shared the joys of seeing a ministry program come together in a church, as well as the frustrations over churches' lack of interest or inability to see that there is any real need. Large, popular churches with over thirty support groups have cancelled meeting after meeting with volunteers of disability ministries.

So, if for some reason the response of your church is not all that you hoped for, don't take it personally. As Luke 10:2 says, "He told them, 'The harvest is plentiful, but the workers are few. Ask the Lord of the harvest, therefore, to send out workers into his harvest field.'" The harvest is plentiful, but there are times churches are not even aware that they have a harvest waiting.

Use this book as a practical tool

As I guide you through the steps of planning your mission and preparing for your group, you will find many things to do and notes you may wish to take. I encourage you to grab both a pen and highlighter and mark this book up so it is functional for you to use and easy to reference in the future. You will find in the appendix a checklist, forms, and example documents that can make it helpful to plan what you would like your illness/pain small group to look like and what needs to be done to accomplish this. This is not a checklist where you must mark each item off as it's completed, but rather, something to look over and decide what areas you want to focus on for the next six months, the next year, etc. It provides a place for you to keep track of your areas of interest as you are reading through the book, on the different things that you may be considering doing, soon or at some point. You may wish to flip to the Appendix now to see what it looks like.

If God says "wait"

If you feel God is saying "No" or "Not now" don't consider it a defeat, but rather just early preparation for the path He may lead you down in the future. Or perhaps you just feel overwhelmed by it all and you don't feel motivated to move forward. That is okay. Even people with the deepest stirring in their heart for illness ministry will still find hurdles to jump over and frustrations in the process, so don't move forward out of guilt or obligation. Having a pastor tell you that the church won't have a HopeKeepers group unless you lead it because "no one else has volunteered to do it" is *not* God calling you to this at this time. Save yourself some heartache and just put this book aside for the time being.

If you feel God saying "yes" then rejoice! And when you feel yourself thinking, "Uh . . but what about. . ." just moments later, don't worry unnecessarily. I hope through this book I can clear up some of those reservations. If God creates a passion for this minstry in you, I hope that I can be one of the tools that God uses to equip you so that you can be the best leader and advocate for the person standing beside you today at the bank as well as the woman sitting next to you in the pew. Millions of people are hurting and just waiting for someone to tell them, "I understand" – and they want to hear it from someone who really does.

> "We had 12 people at our first meeting last night. I just wanted to run somewhere and fall on my face before the Lord—it was so awesome! We had one gal that who unsaved and an older lady that was just a blast— she started right off with a joke about pain (she left him at home.) Later he came and joined us and we all laughed. She was just a sweetie. I think that they left with a different focus and hope in Jesus. There was a genuine feeling of love and compassion among the whole group. We had a gentleman come that has Parkinson's disease-- he was so precious. Some were in just so much pain… I really believe that God allowed me to experience this pain, so I could relate to those who were hurting. I didn't try to fake it. I told them that I was in a lot of pain, but that my Lord was there with me all the way."
> Maggie

Wherever you are at in regards to chronic illness ministry, I hope this book offers you practical tools as well as personal encouragement. Here is a scripture that I read years ago and it felt like a personal prayer I would offer to anyone who is leading a small group for those with chronic illness or pain:

"This service that you perform is not only supplying the needs of God's people but is also overflowing in many expressions of thanks to God. Because of the service by which you have proved yourselves, men will praise God for the obedience that accompanies your confession of the gospel of Christ, and for your generosity in sharing with them and with everyone else. And in their prayers for you their hearts will go out to you, because of the surpassing grace God has given you. Thanks be to God for His indescribable gift" (2 Corinthians 9:12-15).

It is my *prayer* that this book will find its way into the hands of someone who has a passion to make a difference, someone who will step forward to lead their church into becoming a refuge for people with chronic illness as the following person below has.

"I have been talking to my pastor about leading a group such as this and he is all for it. When I was healthy and ministering full-time, I hardly even noticed sick people. Now I can't wait to help them. The Lord has given me a vision!" — Annie

It is my *hope* that when you are done with this book, if you are still considering beginnning a small group a ministry, you feel more equipped in understanding the background of faith/medicine/illness and ministry and are therefore, more aware of how to minister to those who live with chronic illness.

And after you have read the book, continue to spend time in prayer, seeking the Lord's answer if this is to be your calling at this time in your life

"The typical American pastor struggles to make small groups work. Each small gain made in small group life is a hard-fought battle."
Randall G. Neighbour
The Naked Truth About Small Group Ministry

"God whispers in our pleasures, speaks in our conscience, but shouts in our pain. It is His megaphone to rouse a deaf world"
C.S. Lewis

"Should you choose to suffer? No, but choose to get in positions of love which in all likelihood will require suffering . . . don't look for pain – but look for people in pain . . . look at the cost and you embrace the cost"
John Piper

"God never simply buries our dead and broken dreams because He'd be burying our hearts along with our dreams. One of two positive things will happen. Either the dream will become fertilizer for something even better, or the Lord will give me the gumption and oomph to bring my dream to fruition. I can't lose either way!"
Noni Joy Tari

"Some say 'If only my fears and doubts will leave then I will get to work.' But instead you should get to work and then your fears and doubts will leave."
Dwight L. Moody

CHAPTER 3

Where are all the chronic illness small group ministries?

> "Traditionally, the experience of serious illness has been approached in two ways: (1) a gloomy perspective of resignation, self-denial, and helplessness, or (2) a Pollyanna approach that denies altogether that there has been a real trauma. Both of these perspectives distort and disguise the reality of chronic illness."[1]

You are about to embark on changing tradition! The logical first step would be to look around for other chronic illness support groups that are in churches, see how they are functioning, and maybe meet with the leaders. Some people have had the advantage of being able to do this, but you may be surprised to not find an abundance of these groups. In fact, I have rarely found churches that have considered starting such a group—even if they have support group environments for the divorced, caregiver, infertile, and more.

Early on in my ministry I spoke on the telephone with a young man in a wheelchair who lived in San Diego county. He simply needed a ride to church and wondered if I knew of any churches that could provide transportation. When he told me where he lived I assured him that there was a very large church nearby that I was sure would have an accessible transportation ministry. After all, the church had their

44

services televised each week and the pastor was well known around the world as an author, speaker, and radio host.

I called the church and asked the receptionist what kind of transportation was available to church, especially for a person in a wheelchair. I expected her to say, "Yes, of course. We have a van that could pick him up." Instead, I was surprised when she said "Uh. . . no. What do you mean exactly?" And when I tried to explain, sure that she had somehow misunderstood my question, she only said "We don't have any kind of ministry like that. I've never even thought of such a thing." After I insist that she ask around and call me back, she did so, only to tell me, no, they didn't have any kind of transportation available for someone in a wheelchair, but that it was "an interesting idea."

An interesting idea? It was then I began to realize that ministering to those who live a chronic illness or disability was not a priority for most churches — even those we call the "mega-churches." I had assumed that any church with a budget over a million dollars would have at least one or two handicapped accessible vans available.

Since then, the Barna Group, the leading research organization focused on the intersection of faith and culture, found that when studying the priorities of churches, "the largest churches studied were far more likely than smaller congregations to prioritize evangelism and outreach – which may explain their growth. However, larger churches were also *those least likely to mention congregational care ministries* as a priority."[2]

Why are there so few illness or pain ministry groups with a Christian slant that embrace the issues of living with a chronic condition? Let's take a brief look at the history of how faith and illness or disability have interceded.

A brief history

Historically, disability and ministry are no strangers. Religious and charitable societies have always assisted the disabled with humane care and financial support. Many hospitals were birthed from the foundations of religious organizations.

However, even in the world of academia, the study of disability/illness and religion has not been adequately researched. These are a few comments from those who have written articles for *The Disability Quarterly*.

- "Disability within diverse religious, cultural, and historical contexts have only very recently begun to be explored."[3]
- "Religious stories of people with disabilities... are a largely untapped resource for researchers."[4]
- "Historically, the experience of people with disabilities has been an untapped source for theology, often even theology related to disability."[5]
- "The impact of religion and spirituality in the lives of people with disabilities and their family members has been insufficiently investigated."[6]

With the academic world declining in interest or deeming this combination of topics unnecessary, or disinteresting is it any surprise that the media outlets hesitate to publish books on the subject, write magazine articles, and establish such ministries? Let's take a closer look at why there is a shortage of chronic illness ministries.

Western medicine has de-valued the significance of faith

It comes as no surprise that the medical establishment has its own sense of values, and it is rarely interested in expanding those values to include the opinions of religious professionals and patients. "Religious professionals have not always been allowed to evaluate the spiritual needs of people in crisis, much less minister to these needs," writes Blair and Blair in *Pastoral Counselors/Religious Professionals and People with Disabilities.* "This has begun to change as spiritual strength and the power of faith become more apparent as aids in healing, but it is still not uncommon for the spiritual counsel to be ignored altogether or, at best, consulted as an afterthought."[7]

This attitude can easily be witnessed in the statement of Yale psychologist, Seymour B. Sarason, a stated in his address before the Americans Psychological Association in 1992:

> "I think I am safe in assuming that the bulk of the membership of the American Psychological Association would, if asked, describe themselves as agnostic or atheist. I'm also safe in assuming that any one or all of the ingredients of the religious worldview are of neither personal nor professional interest to most psychologists. . . Indeed, if we learn that someone is devoutly religious, or even tends in that direction, we look upon that person with puzzlement, often concluding that psychologist obviously had or has personal problems."[8]

Though this may make us sigh in frustration, Dr. Harold Koenig is a breath of fresh air. Koenig is one of today's chief advocates for doing research and presenting his findings to not just professionals, but also lay people, on the relationship between faith and health. He is founder and former director of Duke University's Center for the Study of Religion, Spirituality and Health, and is founding Co-Director of the current Center for Spirituality, Theology and Health at Duke University Medical Center. He has published extensively in the fields of mental health, geriatrics, and religion, with close to 350 scientific peer-reviewed articles and book chapters and nearly 40 books in print or in preparation.[9]

Many of his books are appropriate for the average person to read and if you wish to learn more on the subject of health and faith I whole-heartedly recommend them. His studies and findings are the foundation for the scientific proof we have today that faith does make a difference in how one copes and responds to his chronic illness, acute illness, or pain. Below Koenig explains his findings on how health experts view faith and its influence on our medical state from his book *Is Religion Good for Your Health?: The Effects of Religion on Physical and Mental Health:*

> "A significant number of mental health experts have argued that religious beliefs and practices are neurotic, maladaptive, and foster the development of guilt, depression, and other mental disorders. . . Primary care physicians and other medical professionals, while less forceful in their negative opinions of religion influences than their psychiatric colleagues, nevertheless largely see religion as irrelevant to health and the delivery of good healthcare."[10]

There have been gradual changes in this attitude as organizations like the International Center for the Integration of Health and Spirituality (formerly the National Institute of Health Research, NIHR), have taken strides in researching the relationship between spirituality and health. The late Dr. David Larson, former president of NIHR co-authored the article "Religion and Spirituality in Medicine: Research and Education" that appeared in the September 3, 1997 issue of the *Journal of the American Medical Association.*
The article emphasizes how research has shown that doctors should start paying more attention to spiritual issues and the spirituality of their patients. Dr. Larson said, "Reporting these

findings in a respected journal like *JAMA* sends physicians a message that religion is a health factor that they need to take seriously."[11] It has taken a long time to get to this point, but faith is beginning to be recognized in the medical arena.

- Does this mean that the doctors across the country are asking their patients to join them in prayer? *It's unlikely.*
- Do these changes signify that your doctor will be more tolerant of your religious beliefs? *Very possibly.*
- Will this research see the emergence of health ministries and chronic illness/pain ministries? *We have yet to find out.*

The "church" has evaded disability issues

The church has been involved with the disabled community for centuries, and yet only recently has the disabled community been able to emerge and speak for themselves. In the past, due to a variety of assumptions, the disabled population was given little intellectual credibility, and others spoke "about them" (not for them).

Although churches may have good intentions when it comes to ministering to those who live with illness or disability, the church body is made up of individuals who are influenced by society and our social culture. It is only natural that these individuals cope with circumstances in human ways which may not always be tactful or even spiritually correct.

> "I have had eight major back surgeries over the past twelve years with various knee blow-outs and hernias. I have traveled the church wilderness and more often then not was condemned by well-meaning believers who did not know His Word. People tend to believe that the Bible says God wants this flesh to be

comfortable and have everything it desires. I could not find this translation." — Willie

Joni and Friends, the internation disability ministry of Joni Eareckson Tada, hired DMT, Inc. to do extensive study to better understand how we are or are not meeting the needs and communicating with those who live with a disability. Their findings were as follows:

- Awareness of disability issues is increasing, but it is increasing slowly and unevenly among communities. Physical accessibility due to the impact of regulations governing transportation, signs, ramps, and other forms of access are largely responsible for this awareness.
- The disability community feels "attitudinal accessibility" is of greater concern than physical accessibility.
- The church mirrors society but lags behind in its attitudes in accessibility to the disability community [which] expects better, and is often disappointed with the church's response.
- The disability community wants more volunteer-based programs and services. The primary characteristics required for volunteers are availability, reliability, and interpersonal skills.[12]

So, to put it bluntly, there is great room for improvement in how the church can: (1) Take a sincere look inward and ask themselves "What would Jesus do?" And then ask, "Are we doing this to the best of our ability?" And if the answer is yes, or it becomes "yes" over a period of time, the church can (2) make it a priority to improve their communication skills to those with disabilities or chronic illnesses; they must communicate how they would like to *not* only serve them, but make them a part of the church body, which includes providing them with opportunities *to* serve and be involved—not just *be* served.

Warren Wiersbe, Christian author of *The Bumps are What You Climb On*, once said "Nothing paralyzes our lives like the attitude that things can never change. We need to remind ourselves that God can change things . . . outlook determines outcome. If we see only the problems, we will be defeated; but if we see the possibilities in the problems, we can have victory."

*"Two are better than one [but] a cord of
three strands is not quickly broken."
Ecclesiastes 4:9-12*

*"Where two or three come together in my
name, there am I with them." Matthew 18:20*

*"We must never minimize the suffering of another.
Scripture" mandate to us is,
'Weep with them that weep.'"
(Romans 12:15, KJV)
Billy Graham*

*"I am not a theologian or a scholar, but I am
very aware of the fact that pain is necessary to all
of us. In my own life, I think I can honestly say
that out of the deepest pain has come the strongest
conviction of the presence of God and the love of God."
Elisabeth Elliot*

*"Some groups connect like a family. A deep bond
develops. Group members sharing hidden pain. Personal
struggles. Anxieties no one else is aware of."*
Bill Search, Simple Small Groups

CHAPTER 4

The benefits of small group ministry

Support groups have become places of refuge for people. Churches have come to recognize that their members have a deep desire to share not only their emotional struggles, (as would be appropriate in a secular support group atmosphere), but people also yearn for a place where the spiritual beliefs they are grappling with is an appropriate and even welcome topic. To fully have any "journey of recovery" Jesus needs to be the crust, the foundation, not just the salt that is sprinkled on top for flavor.

What are the benefits of a small group for those with illness and how can you lead it if you are ill? Let's take a closer look at this.

Small groups can address any topic

Whether it's called a small group, support group, home fellowship, life group, cell group, or care group, churches have been taking steps to address personal needs by offering supportive groups within the church community. Although there are secular community groups where people who live with issues of alcoholism, eating disorders, sexual abuse, divorce, blended families, and addiction are able to find a supportive environment, we need more settings that allow us to discuss our spiritual strengths and weaknesses, questions and concerns. If we refrain from depending on God's power that is available to us through Jesus Christ, we will end up surrendering to the pressures that surround us.

Dale S. Ryan explains in a chapter he authored, "Customizing Personal Ministry" in *Building Your Church through Counsel and Care,* one of advantages of support groups in churches: "People often will come to support groups who will not accept care extended in any other way. Because care is offered by people who share that particular struggle, people see support groups as safe places to receive care."[1]

Many churches have used small groups as the foundation for the large church body itself where it can be hard for intimacy to occur on a typical Sunday morning service that thousands may attend.

For example, Saddleback Church, in Saddleback, CA has about 20,000 members with nearly forty small groups/ support groups specifically on medical or health-related issues alone. The groups range in topics from families of those with mental illness, to those with illness or pain, caregivers, those dealing with infertility, to parents of kids with special needs.[2]

Their pastor, Rick Warren, is a best-selling author, well known for his life-changing book that has sold over 30 million copies, *A Purpose Driven Life.* Many of his books and resources are developed specifically for small groups or support groups environments. For example, Saddleback Church is the founder of "Celebrate Recovery", a program established in 1991 with the goal of overcoming bad habits like (such as drug addictions) with a twelve-step program, which is based on Christian principles.

In 2009, Rick Warren began another program called "Life's Healing Choices National Campaign." Thousands of churches have joined Saddleback in this 8-week "spiritual growth campaign" based on The Beatitudes. Churches can "help people find freedom from hurts, hang-ups, and habits."[3] On the official website it states the following about kicking off the program: "Many of the leaders were from Celebrate Recovery and they were surprised at the instant openness and trust that the participants showed in their sharing."[4]

While some are critical of Warren for his marketing campaigns to launch new ministry tools, pastors who are looking to meet a need they see in their church are relieved to find all of the materials in one place. It's a toolbox designed to help them do their job better and it's from a source that they can trust and gain pastoral assistance or encouragement themselves when needed.

Healing is a motivation for attendance

Small groups are a tool to connect people with one another in the body of the church and — with attendance, and sometimes repentance — one can be healed of whatever may ail them while enjoying the fellowship of others who are on a similar journey. So it stands to reason that a chronic illness small group ministry would fit into this organizational structure of groups, right? Why is it that they are often difficult to find in your typical church?

In my opinion, there is a keyword that jumps out in the description above: *Heal.* Many people are attending these various support groups in order to be healed in some way. Whether it be from the stronghold something has over them like alcohol or food, to a relationship burden, such as divorce recovery, the goal is often to be healed of whatever it is that ails them. Whether it be an emotional, a mental, a spiritual healing — or all three — each person comes seeking healing in some way.

Where are all the illness small groups?

If you are wondering why there seem to be few illness support groups in churches, I believe that one reason is this: when churches and other organizations try to minister to the ill, the focus is often that of *physical healing*, not necessarily the emotional or spiritual healing and they feel they are already addressing this need. Why would they need to organize a small group for those with illness when they already have a special service dedicated to healing prayers and the application of the oil? Why would they need a small group for ill people to attend when there is already home visitation ministry for the ill or elderly?

Generally speaking, for the most part, churches earnestly believe they have this area of ministry already covered. They pray for healing every day for those who are ill in their church. They have special prayer meetings among staff. They may send their pastor out to visit someone in the hospital or a parish nurse to an elderly woman's home to fellowship while taking she is taking the church member's blood pressure. Physical healing is nearly always expected unless the person is in their later years and has "had a good life"and hope is surrendered over to God's will.

When the prayers for a physical healing are not answered, then what? The unanswered prayer can be interpreted as a sign from God that one of the following has occurred:

- The person with the illness lacked faith
- The person with the illness has unconfessed sin in his or her life
- The person with the illness has not asked for forgiveness
- The prayer was not done correctly
- Someone who prayed lacked faith

- It's not God's timing. "We'll try again at our next prayer meeting in six months."

Unfortunately, the person who needs the most support and encouragement is often left feeling condemned and even more isolated than before she was prayed for. She's been told, "You are such a good person. I know God will heal you." So when God doesn't, does that mean she *isn't* a good person after all? If God doesn't care about her, and people in the church are judgmental or ambiguous, where can she turn?

She can turn to a small group, a refuge for people who want to live joyfully, not just survive, with chronic illness. William Gurnall once said, "Hope fills the afflicted soul with such inward joy and consolation, that it can laugh while tears are in the eye, sigh and sing all in a breath; it is called 'the rejoicing of hope' as in Hebrews 3:6." This is the kind of atmosphere one will find at a HopeKeepers group: tears, but also rejoicing in hope.

> "Being able to express myself without being afraid of judgment, because others with chronic illness would better understand where I am coming from, would be all the motivation I would need to join a group." — Bonnie

Christians oftentimes feel isolated in their pain. They aren't allowed to discuss their faith at medical support group meetings because someone may be offended. And unfortunately, too often Christian friends say things that hurt. If you have a chronic illness it would not be presumptuious for me to say ou have likely heard at least one of these in some manner:

- "If you had more faith. . ."
- "Maybe God is trying to teach you something. . ."

- "If you just try to think positive, the pain will go away."
- "You focus on it too much!"
- "Have you been praying about this enough?"
- "What did you do to deserve this?"

Even when these comments are made in a joking way or a sarcastic tone that is meant to be light-hearted, the message is still clear to the person who is ill: <u>You</u> must be doing <u>something</u> to prevent your healing from occurring.

In a Christ-based chronic illness support group, such as HopeKeepers groups, although people are encouraged to talk about the frustrations that they encounter along their chronic illness journey, the focus of the group is on living a life that is, to the best of our ability, glorifying to God. It is on embracing hope, regardless of the pharmaceutical company's research or our nation's healthcare plan. It is on the pain-free heaven that we will one day experience. Although our days may be filled with flares, stiffness, breathing difficulties, or endless headaches, we are encouraged by our faith in God who has a reason for every drop of pain that we experience, even though we may never understand the reason.

So who wants to lead a group of people who have gone through such an experience? Who amongst us feels qualified to lead such a group? Who of us can explain to a person why God is not healing her? Does the leader of a chronic illness small group pray for healing or help? Function or faith? Answered prayer or patience?

Although it can sound overwhelming, you may be surprised to find yourself saying, "I could do this!" or "This just may work." Elbert Hubbard, a writer from the 1800s once said, "God will not look you over for medals degrees or diplomas, but for scars." Despite the doubts you may have, God has given you all the credentials you need if this is His purpose for you.

What if I become too ill to lead the group?

There will always be the possibility that you may become too ill to lead the group, but that possibility exists with any group leader, healthy or ill. None of us have any guarantee that something in our life won't cause our abilities or priorities to shift. We must surrender all of those "what ifs" over to God.

And if you are reading this book, I tend to think you likely don't let a little pain hold you back from doing as many day-to-day activities as you can. My advice is don't allow your illness to hold you back from experiencing the joy that God has in store for you. All of our lives are unpredictable. If you wait until you "feel better…" most memories in life will never get a chance to be made. And while you are feeling your worst is when even *you* may most need the encouragement of others. The fact that you can already envision the day you turn the group over to another leader can even be considered wise.

"Just as Jesus realized, a true leader will not be with his or her followers at all times, and there will come a time when the leader will leave this world forever," says Briner & Prichard in their book *More Leadership Lessons of Jesus.* "Such a leader's goal is to enable followers to function as well as possible in the absence of the leader, whether the absence is temporary or permanent. Good leaders discuss this openly and unself-consciously, as Jesus did. Short-sighted leaders build and execute a program based on the fallacy that they will always be there. Their program only works in an optimum way when they are present and the followers serve through the leader." This may be a good quote, in fact, to read to your church leadership team when they ask you about your limitations.

I don't expect you to have all of the answers. I don't expect you to never miss a meeting. I don't expect you to have a clean house. (How could I even consider all of these when I cannot even do them?) But I do know that God assures us "In quietness and trust is your strength" (Isaiah 30:15). It's okay to be a leader who is not full of strength and who is unable to bark out directions with confidence all the time. Sometimes our strength can be discovered in our quiet presence.

Open your heart up to becoming a "wounded healer." A wounded healer is one portrayed by 2 Corinthians 1:4: "[God] comforts us in all our troubles, so that we can comfort those in any trouble with the comfort we ourselves have received from God."

I don't know why God has given you chronic illness or physical pain in your life. Perhaps you are searching for the reason. Consider the fact that 2 Corinthians 1:4 may be His purpose, and a small group may be the way to carry out His plan for your life.

Depending on the illness you have, you may occasionally be unable to attend the group or you may go through a season of weeks or even months where you are not able to prepare a lesson or possibly attend. I strongly encourage you to find a co-leader who can help you in all areas of your ministry, including stepping up to lead at the last minute when you are unable to do so.

You may also want to consider yourself not necessarily the "leader" of the group, but rather a facilitator. After your group has met for a few months, depending on the personalities and abilities of the people in your group, ask them to each be responsible for some area of helping the group function. Perhaps, someone knows a few people who would be willing to come and do a presentation for your group on a particular topic of interest. Or, if you have people who feel comfortable leading a Bible study, you may want to distribute the responsibilities of the five lessons to five different people.

HopeKeepers leader, Jessica, shares what has occurred when she has been too ill to lead:

> "While I haven't found an official co-facilitator, the group is bonding so quickly, I'm sure someone will step up when I'm not there. I actually feel like once we get started, the group kind of leads itself. I'm being blessed in so many ways with this ministry." -Jessica

In this day of technology, you can still stay connected to group members even when you are not feeling well. You may be able to call them during the group meeting and be put on speaker phone to say hello and for the closing prayer. If you and another member are technology savvy (or you have a teenager in the house), you may want to learn more about Skype, the free program that allows you to see the person you are talking to on the computer screen; it's like a free phone call but with visuals. (Some days this is a good thing; some days, we'd rather hide behind a normal telephone!)

You may be afraid of what will happen to your schedule if you are not there or if you are unable to fully participate in a group meeting as planned. Remember that God's idea of equipping you for a mission or the completion of it may likely be very different than yours. What you define as "success" may be quite different than God's meaning of success.

So allow me emphasize again that this is God's ministry; therefore, if you are seeking His will and praying "Thy will be done" God's will *will* be done . . . but the likelihood that it will be done in the way you had originally envisioned, is much less likely that you would like to admit. Don't be afraid of sharing your weaknesses and vulnerabilities. It was the meeting that I confessed to the members of my group that I was exhausted and had cried on my way in the car that I believe they most related to me and began to trust me. They knew that I was walking alongside them and not there to offer them placating advice.

How can I be the best leader possible despite my illness?

To lead a small group, you should be faithful, available, and teachable. Oswald Chambers once said, "God will never reveal more truth about Himself until you have obeyed what you know already." In other words, when God prompts you to do something, don't waste any time complaining, explaining, questioning or basically, disobeying.

Instead, remain close to the Father and stick your toe in the water. God won't push you off any diving boards before teaching you to swim, but He knows it's pointless to teach you the backstroke if you won't even get wet.

5 characteristics of effective Bible discussion leaders

1. *The characteristic of obedience*

   If you are considering becoming a leader of a small group, there are three things, which you must be right in relationship to. These are: (1) God; (2) God's Word; and (3) God's people and persons in position to authority.

2. *The characteristic of prayer*

   People are looking for someone to pray for them and with them. Prayer is a vital part of our relationship with God.

3. *The characteristic of belief*

   We need to have a faith that is enthusiastic. Without faith, we are unable to please God and therefore are of no direct benefit to others.

4. ***The characteristic of compassion combined with clear communication***
    Scripture tells us to speak the truth in love (Ephesians 4:1).
5. ***The characteristic of study and preparation***
    2 Timothy explains how leaders must be teachable in order to correctly handle the word of truth.

I have read many books, including the scriptures, to try to be the best leader I can be. Here are a couple of quotes I'd like to pass on to you.

> "I am a shepherd. It wasn't something I chose as a business profession. It was something I could not escape! John 15:16 reminds me: 'You did not choose Me but I chose you, and appointed you that you would go and bear fruit, and that your fruit would remain.'"[5]

> "People don't expect their leaders to be able to do everything. What they do expect is authenticity. People will respect you more when you're willing to admit your weaknesses."[6]

Being a leader means completely surrendering your plans and your agenda over to the Father and then prayerfully waiting for Him to lead you in the right direction one step at a time.

*"It was character that got us out of bed,
commitment that moved us into action, and
discipline that enabled us to follow through."*
Zig Ziglar

*"You have to live with the people to
know their needs, and you have to
live with God to know how to solve them"*
John C. Maxwell

*"Do not believe that any man will become a
physician unless he walks the hospitals. And I
am sure that no one will become a minister or
comforter unless he lies in the hospital as well as
walks through it, and has to suffer himself."*
Charles Spurgeon

*"If you have courage, you will influence people based
on your convictions. If you lack courage, you will
influence people based on your comfort zones. Courage
will take you anywhere you believe God is leading you.
Without courage, you will go where you are comfortable."*
Wayne Schmidt

*"'She did what she could do—Mark 14' is written
on the tombstone of Fanny Crosby, blind composer
of over four thousand hymns. Don't have anxious
thoughts about the high stakes involved in Christian
service. Just ask for the Spirit's help and do what
you are able to do. Jesus will think it's beautiful."*
Joni Eareckson Tada, Pearls of Great Price

CHAPTER 5

Leading a small group when you are ill

The time has come where you are asking yourself, "Should I really consider this? *Can* I do this?" You may find it reassuring to know that the people who lead HopeKeepers groups rarely feel like they are bursting with unlimited energy or that they spiritually have it all together. Thankfully, God has never required perfection in order to give us a project with purpose. Rick Warren once said, "If you're alive, there's a purpose for your life." So take a deep breath and remember that it's not about perfection—it's about providing a place where people with illness can get together, pray for one another's needs, and grow closer to the Father.

Anticipate addressing your fears and concerns

It is likely something will not work out exactly as you had hoped or imagined. Maybe the evening of your first meeting you arrive at the church only to discover the room you are using is locked up and you cannot get in touch with anyone. Or the janitors set up the cold metal folding chairs, when the pastor in charge specifically had said he would make sure your room had the padded chairs to add comfort. Perhaps the person who said she would bring healthy snacks decided at the last minute to bring soda and cupcakes, and now most of the people who are attending cannot eat anything. Maybe you stopped by the church office the day of the meeting to pick up the Bible studies being sent to you, only to discover that the secretary locked them into a drawer so they wouldn't get lost and now you can't reach her by phone.

The situation can resemble a woman's wedding plans. She knows that it's likely something will not turn out exactly as she had planned, but when the day rolls around she can choose to allow that to ruin it or she can go with the flow and hope for the best. You have the added benefit of know that God really *is* in control and these are just minor inconveniences.

Turning our heart's desires over to God

Whatever God wants to have happen there at that meeting, will happen. This includes a broken coffee pot or a parade of cars to your home because the meeting room is locked up. These unexpected disruptions, however, will not change the plans He has. Remember, "Many are the plans in a man's heart, but it is the Lord's purpose that prevails" (Proverbs 19:21). So take a deep breath and turn your anxieties over to Him.

Proverbs 19:2 tells us "It is not good to have zeal without knowledge, nor to be hasty and miss the way." God actually *does* know your plans . . . but He is going to make *His* purpose prevail, in His timing. This can actually feel like a bit of a bummer because our plans seem so good! And your plans are likely God-honoring, compassionate, and send a message of understanding to those attending your meeting (like you know they need comfortable seats and can't eat sugar). But God will over-rule even the best of plans we make in order for *His* plans to take place. So relax. You are in good hands, even when things go awry.

Revelation 3:8 says, "I know your deeds. See, I have placed before you an open door that no one can shut. I know that you have little strength, yet you have kept My word and have not denied My name." As you are considering starting a small group or getting ready to take something to the church's leadership team, remember that the outcome is *God's* decision. God knows your deeds –and all about your *little* strength! Is it not amazing that this scripture tells us that God is placing an open door before us that no person can shut— even though He knows all about our little strength?

In this chapter we are going to discuss some of these fears or concerns you may have. These include:

- I don't have any experience
- I haven't led a group for a long time
- I don't have much scripture memorized
- Is this something God wants me to do?
- I am not sure I have the right motives
- What if no one comes?
- It sounds like a lot of work
- What if people have needs I can't handle?
- How do I set healthy boundaries?

There will be times that you don't feel like you know what you are doing. I do understand that it can be scary to step outside of your comfort zone and you likely will feel moments of awkwardness. God often places us in situations where we feel in over our head so we *must* rely on Him. Hebrews 11:8 says, "By faith, Abraham, when called to go to a place he would later receive as his inheritance, obeyed and went, *even though he did not know where he was going"* (emphasis added). God is fully aware of your abilities—and your weaknesses. It is through your willingness to follow Him despite feeling less than perfect or not knowing exactly where you are going, that He will be able to do what He wants to do with this ministry. Corrie Ten Boom once said, "Worry is a cycle of inefficient thoughts whirling around a center of fear." Worry is understandable, but truly rather pointless. Betty describes what her small group has taught her:

> "Our HopeKeepers group has shown me how to transform Parkinson's [Disease] from a source of self-pity to a means to draw closer to God. Through study of [Lisa] Copen's books and other Christian literature, I have learned that trusting and obeying God is the best way to disarm fear--the core of all suffering. The group allows me to comfortably share feelings and aid other Christians with chronic illness. HopeKeepers has been a place for me to put into perspective my disability. It's helped me to cope, with more spiritual understanding, on a day-to-day level." –Betty

I like how she explains, "I have learned that trusting and obeying God is the best way to disarm fear." Zanina Jacinto, who lives with multiple sclerosis and is the author of *And He Will Lift You Up*, shares how she overcomes fears when God is leading her down an unknown path:

> "God tells us in Psalm 119:105 that "[His] Word is a lamp to [our] feet and a light for [our] path." It's pitch black. God gives you a lamp and places it at your feet. What relief! Now you can see! But at that moment, you realize that you can only see a few feet in front of you. Everything around you is still black. A lamp at our feet only guides us step by step. The path is revealed as we take the steps that we can see, trusting that we will know which way to go as His lamp lights the way. Remember, fear is the enemy of faith. If I feel afraid and refuse to move where God leads me, I go nowhere and my fear likely intensifies."[1]

I don't have any experience

Do you feel ill equipped? You are in good company. Henry Blackaby, author *of Experiencing God*, explains in his book how people who step forward in faith and follow God's direction to be involved in an area ministry which is not in their comfort zone, will find that they are equipped spiritually in time. He says:

> "[God] will provide an equipping to match the new task. That is why there are people who, over the years, have discovered that their 'spiritual gifts' seem to change. The reason? Their assignment shifted, so the Holy Spirit equips them to accomplish their new task. If God merely provided us with a gift, we would tend to place our confidence in the gift rather than in Him. But since the Holy Spirit does the work through us, we must continually rely upon our relationship with Him if we are to be effective in the ministry He gives us.

> Conversely, if we refuse to obey what God asks us to do, the Holy Spirit will not equip us. We don't need to be equipped for something we refuse to do. Our divine enabling always comes as we obey what God tells us to do—never before our obedience. Focus your attention on hearing God's call to an assignment which is His invitation for you to join Him. When you adjust your life to Him and obey Him, the Holy Spirit will work in you, enabling you to accomplish what God desires."2

It can be a bit intimidating to put yourself in the position of leading a group when you have so few answers about why people are suffering or how exactly God is being glorified through it. But Scripture tells us to not be afraid. "Get yourself ready! Stand up and say to them whatever I command you. Do not be terrified by them, or I will terrify you before them. "(Jeremiah 1:17) In other words, if God is telling you to go for it then you better go for it. C. Gene Wilkes emphasizes in his book *Jesus on Leadership, Discovering the Secrets if Servant Leadership from the Life of Christ*, "God didn't go looking for leaders. God looked for obedient people whom He then formed into leaders."[3]

I haven't led a group for a long time

Perhaps it has been many years since you have been in a leadership position. Those who live with chronic illness may have once been very active in their church, community, a nonprofit organization, or their children's school. But due to the nature of chronic illness and the frequent changes in the severity of pain you will experience, it can be hard to pledge yourself to a position of leadership, where people are expecting you to be able to fulfill the responsibilities that you have committed to. I hear from people who are still grieving the loss of having to drop out of the church choir or resign from teaching the children's Sunday School class. Just when you may need a distraction from the pain and to have the arms of the church body wrapped around you, you end up having to leave the positions that gave you an outlet for your gifts and the fellowship with other volunteers.

The good news is that you can use your gift of withstanding suffering as part of your new ministry involvement. I had the opportunity to share my testimony in the book *The Transforming Power of Story*: "The blessings I have been given through my chronic illness, from the tangible to the spiritual, are gifts that came in the ugly gift wrap of illness, but gifts I would still never exchange for my health."[4] Your illness may not have been the way you desired to find God's calling for your life, but in this situation, your illness has the refreshing ability to be considered an asset!

Do not feel as though you are solely responsible for a 90-minute program of worship, Bible study, discussion, snacks and counseling. You can follow a Bible study, have guest speakers, go on "field trips," have fun fellowship time, or even have an evening with friends or spouses. You will have the freedom to develop your group to best meet the needs of those who are involved. I recommend a balance of the above ideas and will share more about them later.

I don't have much scripture memorized

If you are feeling God's nudge to move forward and begin a small group ministry but you feel as though you don't know your Bible inside and out, it can be intimidating to be around people who seem to be able to recite not only all the books of the Bible, but complete chapters of Scripture. Have you ever been in a setting where someone says, "Turn to the book of Jeremiah" and you suddenly feel a sense of panic, as everyone seems to be quickly turning to the book of Jeremiah? Only . . . you have no idea where the book of Jeremiah is! And to flip to your table of contents in your Bible to find the page number would be a quick disclosure of your lack of spiritual maturity, right?

Do you know that many of us have been in the same position? You do not have to be someone who can recite the books of the Bible backwards and forward or be able to quickly tell someone the exact reference for a scripture when they bring it up. I remember about five years ago I felt as though I was "giving in" and admitting a great defeat in spiritual maturity when I purchased the little sticky page markers with all of the names of the books of the Bible and put them into my Bible so that I could find Scriptures more easily.

Yes, I once has them all memorized, and am actually in the process of doing it again now, as my son is in AWANAs and memorizing them is part of his goal. Consequently, I am learning them again as well. But there won't be a pop quiz on this that you must pass in order to lead the group. The most important thing is that you are always willing to spend a few minutes looking up a scripture for the answers, even if you have to get back to someone in your group later on in the week.[5]

Memorizing scripture will bring you great comfort; especially during the times you are unable to have your Bible with you (like when you are having an MRI!) But God always desires us to focus on Him and His Word—not on our own accomplishments.

1 Peter 5:5b says, "But all of you, leaders and followers alike, are to be down to earth with each other, for—God has had it with the proud, but takes delight in just plain people." God is impressed with your relationship and time spent in fellowship with Him, not how many references you can rattle off to impress people.

I'm not sure if this is something God wants me to do

You may or may not experience a lightning bolt kind of answer from God about how you should proceed. But I do believe that you should have a sense of peace about it that surpasses all of the logistical reasons of why you should not do it. Pray . . . pray . . . and then pray some more.

There will always be challenges, and there will definitely be times where you feel in over your head or simply

---

[5] A wonderful tool is www.BibleGateway.com that can help you find a scripture in any translation by searching via keyword, topic or reference.

exhausted. However, if you feel this is something that God desires you to do, nothing will be able to give you the same sense of passion and joy that you will feel when you are what many describe as "in the center of God's will."

To understand more fully if starting a chronic illness ministry is something that God wants you to do, I recommend asking yourself the following questions and reading the Scriptures referenced.

- Do you have a growing and maturing relationship with the Lord? (See John 15:5)
- Do you have a sense of calling from the Lord to serve people? (See John 21:15-17)
- Do you have a vision for building up future leaders? (See 2 Timothy 2:2)
- Do you want to glorify the Lord with whatever you do? (See Col. 3:23)
- Do you want to bear fruit in your life? (See John 15:8)
- Do you want to shepherd others and be an example? (See 1 Peter 5:2)

I am not sure I have the right motives

This is a good time to sit back and reflect on your spiritual journey during your lifetime so far, and where it overlaps with your chronic illness experience. Why exactly do you want to lead this group? Author John Maxwell says, "It's lonely at the top, so you better know why you are there."

If you live with a chronic illness, chances are that you have felt like many things have been taken away from you. I remember my first experience with this emotion. I saw a delivery driver carry in some boxes to where I worked and I realized that I would no longer ever have the career option to be a delivery driver. I did not have dreams of being a delivery driver, but up until that point I believed I had the physical ability to do the job if I put forth the effort. We often feel as though we have lost the ability to simply have choices in our life.

So this is a good time to truthfully examine what your motivation is for wanting to lead a group. Psalm 139:23 says, "Search me, O God, and know my heart; test me and know my anxious thoughts." It takes a wise (and brave!) person to truly pray, "Search me, O God," but He will reveal to you the areas on your life in which you do need His help or to ask for forgiveness.

For example, most of us are somewhere in the cycle of grief, whether it be a denial, bargaining, anger, or acceptance. If you are currently living in the state of anger about your illness, even if you put forth a great deal of effort in trying to remain positive, your anger will still seep through and be a part of your leadership style. Now would not be the best time to put yourself in a leadership position where you are trying to encourage others on how to effectively live with a chronic illness.

Also, if you are feeling a great deal of frustration with your church because you feel they "refuse to acknowledge the needs of people who live with chronic illness," you may need to sit back and wait until you have a different attitude. If you feel angry that the church has not responded to you in the way that you believe they should, and you are "by golly going to change that so no one else has to go through the hell that you have gone through," this is not the time to go to your pastor and explain to him why he should allow you to start a chronic illness ministry.

Instead, you should have a mindset that you have perhaps discovered a place in your church where there is a missed ministry opportunity, and you would like to use the experiences and gifts that God has given you to help the church increase their outreach to the chronically ill.

Look back at your answers to the questions in the section above about your relationship with the Lord and your sense of calling for this ministry. Did you answer yes to all of the questions? If so, you can be assured that you probably have the right motives for wanting to participate in small group leadership. If you answered no to some of them, you should examine your motives a little closer.

Do you want to lead a small group:

- *For self-exaltation?* The Bible says, "Let another praise you, and not yourself," (Proverbs 27:2). Ken Blanchard, Christian author of numerous books on business, including *The One Minute Manager,* says that our priorities become mixed up when we began to spell the word God E-G-O. "EGO" stands for "edging God out."
- *To feel important or for the prestige?* We are not here to please man, but to please God. Look at your reasons for desiring prestige (1 Thess. 2:4-6).
- *Because someone has pressured you to do it?* Don't get involved with something that you don't have a passion for, because you won't last and you will not be an effective leader. 1 Peter 5:2 says "Be shepherds of God's flock that is under your care, serving as overseers—not because you must, but because you are willing, as God wants you to be; not greedy for money, but eager to serve."

According to Wilkes, "Biblical leadership always begins with a God-sized mission in the form of a call by God. Those commissioned by God to carry out that call become leaders because they first follow God's call. Biblical servant leadership never begins with the individual's wishes to better the world or attain a personal goal. Servant leadership finds its motive from God's commissioning a person to carry out a divine plan among a group of people."5

What if no one comes?

I will be honest with you . . . there is that possibility — or times when just one person comes. When I first began a HopeKeepers group there was a great deal of interest and excitement around the time of the kickoff. But within a month there was one occasion when I came to the meeting place at the community library, and sat there by myself. Another time, just one woman came, and it was her first visit. It can be embarrassing for us as a leader, to have a new member from the community attend, and then have no one there but us. She and I spent over an hour just chatting and praying though, and as we walked to our cars she said that she had gained a great deal from our time together and she confided that she was a very shy person and likely would not have even spoken out had other people been present. That night I discovered one of the meanings of Proverbs 25:15: "Patient persistence pierces through indifference; gentle speech breaks down rigid defenses." (*The Message*)

As disheartening or discouraging as it can be to sit alone at a meeting with your Bible, study, and a bottle of water, I believe that God uses these moments to accelerate our spiritual growth in a way that may not have happened had we had a roomful of people. Humbly seeking the Lord, and not always getting to experience the glory of a crowd, is part of the building blocks that God uses in creating us to be the leader that He wishes us to be. They say that every good leader has had a mentor. I believe that every authentic leader once stood before an empty room.

It sounds like a lot of work

Organizing and developing a successful small group is not an easy task that you should take on without first considering your investment. You will be committing your time, emotions, and it will stretch any leadership skills you may feel you already have.

> "What I'm struggling with now in the group is dealing with so many personalities. Sometimes I feel like I need to be a trained therapist to do this ministry, but I know the Lord called me to start it." –Judy

Luke 14:28-30 says, "Suppose one of you wants to build a tower. Will he not first sit down and estimate the cost to see if he has enough money to complete it? For if he lays the foundation and is not able to finish it, everyone who sees it will ridicule him, saying, 'This fellow began to build and was not able to finish.'"

In short, Jesus does tell us to wisely count the costs of our choices before making a commitment. You may feel a stirring in your heart for chronic illness ministry and as though you cannot *not* do it. Or you may feel like you see the need but that you are unable to move forward with it right at this time—or maybe never. There should be *no shame* in this whatsoever, nor should you be tempted to move forward simply out of obligation and pressure from those around you.

It is a wise woman who also talks to those around her seeking wisdom. If you are a mom and a wife, for example, leading a group and becoming invested in the lives of people who will have needs will affect your family. Your level of energy (or lack thereof), as well as time, will impact your family too and this should be taken into consideration.

The priorities in our lives should be (1) God; (2) family; (3) and then ministry. It is very easy to blur these lines, especially when we feel like we are doing something so worthy and pleasing to the Lord. However, if your time with God and your family takes a back seat, your ministry, regardless of how many people you are helping, will become fruitless.

On a more positive note, you will find that although a small group leadership role can be a lot of work, it can be the most exhilarating, exciting, fun work you will ever do. You will be around people who show great strength and compassion. You are in a mission field. You will see people who are extremely grateful for the time you are giving them. You will see God at work on a daily basis. Personally, despite how much personal energy and time I have spent on behalf of Rest Ministries, I have continued to do it for many years simply because it is one of the greatest joys I could ever imagine. I feel blessed that the Lord has allowed me to have a ministry rather than just a career.

What if people have needs I can't handle?

The likelihood that people will eventually have a need that you are unable or not equipped to handle is strong. This is a group of people who live with daily illness or pain, and they may not have any family members who live nearby. They may be barely surviving on their finances; friends have drifted away, and they may be experiencing a wide variety of emotions, many of which they have never discussed with any other person. Many people who live with chronic illness also deal with deep depression or other mental health issues.

One of the benefits of having your small group under the administration of the church is that you are able to go to your pastoral staff and ask for help in directing people with needs beyond the scope of your group to the best resources in the church or in the community. If you feel in over your head, or if you feel that a person is at risk of suicide, you have a church that is equipped to step in during emergency situations like this and take over for you.

It can be helpful when you are welcoming people to a new group, or when you give them a welcome packet if they enter the group after it has begun, to explain what the actual purpose of HopeKeepers is and what you are equipped to handle.

> "I think we all want to help in any way we can, but I think HopeKeepers is more for spiritual support and encouragement than physical and financial help. Discussing these things and drawing the lines beforehand might be to the benefit of any group." - Jessica

After it has been decided to start the group, discuss with your pastoral staff that if there are needs outside of your abilities and responsibilities, who should you share them with the at the church? And who should you talk to about it if it is after hours?

For example, if during your meeting a woman reveals that she had been saving up her pain medication and is truly tempted to just take them and end it all to stop the pain, who should you contact?

Or, if someone who is attending your group shares a prayer request that she desperately needs to purchase a scooter for mobility, but is currently unable to afford this, is there someone in the church who should be made aware of this need, in case there is a possibility of the church having a fund set aside for these kind of expenses? It is not your responsibility to go out and organize a fundraiser for this need. However, sometimes by simply making someone else aware of the need, it can be covered. Also, in cases like this, sometimes church members like to know about the need, because they may be able to specify that they would like a particular donation to go to help cover this expense.

> "I got caught up in a situation where a lady without insurance, family, or a car ended up leaning very heavily on my kindness—taking her to the hospital and waiting with her in the Emergency Room on multiple occasions, helping to pay for medications, etc. I wanted to help, but started to feel a bit taken advantage of. So it is very important for a leader and their pastor or whoever is in leadership over them to discuss and decide what the church and leader can and can't do for group members who are in need. I realize we are here to help those in need, but it was a difficult situation and hard for me to draw the line with her when I decided I could not take any more time and money (we scrape by) from my family for her." – Jessica

In the book *Setting Boundaries*, the authors describe what the difference is between helping and enabling.

- *Helping* is doing something for someone that he is not capable of doing himself.
- *Enabling* is doing for someone things that he could and should be doing himself. An enabler is a person who recognizes that a negative circumstance is occurring on a regular basis and yet continues to enable the person with the problem to persist with his detrimental behaviors. [6]

Every person who takes on a role of ministry, whether a formal role as a leader, or an informal role as encourager to a neighbor, must learn to set priorities that are pleasing to God. Romans 12:2 says, "Do not conform any longer to the pattern of this world, but be transformed by the renewing of your mind. Then you will be able to test and approve what God's will is—His good, pleasing and perfect will."

It can be easy to get busy for God! I know how quickly zeal about a new ministry can take over my time and thoughts. Ultimately, however, we realize that we are only human and not only does God not *expect* us to do it all, He doesn't *want* us to do it all! He needs a willing heart, but also a sensible head, as we learn to not put all our time into producing fruit for Him, but also listen and spend time with Him.

You can't do and be all and God doesn't want you to because that is *His* job. Have some special tract or booklets to encourage people that you can drop in the mail. Call if you feel like it and explain you have five minutes to talk because you too are ill. People appreciate transparency.

Be conscious of the whether your resources for the group are *more. . .* or *less* than your responsibilities. Michael C. Mack, author of *The Pocket Guide to Burnout-Free Small Group Leadership: How to Gather a Core Team and Lead from the Second Chair* explains, "In the ideal world," he says, "you as a leader should have an equal amount of (or more) resources compared to your number of responsibilities. When you become frustrated and burned out as a leader, on further inspection you will find that you have far more responsibilities than resources. There are two ways to remedy small group leader burnout: reduce your responsibilities or increase your resources (or both)."[7]

When you are a group leader it can be hard to set healthy boundaries, but knowing what your responsibilities are at the beginning and setting boundaries for yourself, is one of the best steps you can make it maintaining the life and health of the group. "Learning the difference between a concern and a responsibility may save your ministry, your family, and your sanity. If we misdefine concerns as personal responsibilities, it will eventually confuse us and diffuse our energies."[8]

In closing, keep in mind that there will always be reasons or excuses that we try to explain to God. Perhaps Moses is one of the most well-known Biblical men who came up with excuses, some of which we can easily relate to. These are my paraphrases:

- "I don't have any experience in that area." (Exodus 3:11)
- "Who am I that they should listen to me? They will ignore me." (Exodus 3:13)
- "What if they don't believe me?" (Exodus 4:1)
- "I'm not a very good speaker." [Moses may actually have had a stutter, which we could say was a disability] (Exodus 4:10)
- "Can't you find someone else, someone more qualified, and who has not sinned as I have?" (Exodus 4:13)

In each case God upheld His command to Moses and told him his excuses were not going to get Him out of that which God had called him to. Regardless of how painful a new challenge may feel, remember God's promise to you: "For I know the plans I have for you,' declares the Lord, 'plans to prosper you and not to harm you, plans to give you hope and a future.'" (Jeremiah 29:11)

Nancy Groom, author of *From Bondage to Bonding: Escaping Codependency, Embracing Biblical Love* says, "Depending utterly on God for our ultimate well-being is the doorway to intimacy, to a renewed freedom to love, to hurt, to laugh, to make mistakes, to ask forgiveness, to feel our feelings, to start each day new."[9]

*"Leaders among God's people come into leadership
as they are carrying out God's mission/call."
C. Gene Wilkes*

*"Courage would be impossible
in a world without pain."
Lee Strobel*

*"We think we understand another person's struggle
until God reveals the same shortcomings in our lives."
Oswald Chambers*

*"A scar is a wound that has healed. We need to bring
our wounds to Jesus, let Him heal them, and use our
scars for Jesus. Our scars may be our greatest ministry."
Adrian Rogers, pastor, Bellevue Baptist Church*

*"Never doubt that a small group of thoughtful,
committed people can change the world. Indeed, it is the
only thing that ever has." Unknown*

*"Unless commitment is made, there are
only promises and hopes; but no plans."
Peter F. Drucker*

CHAPTER 6

Formulating the purpose of your small group

So now that you have examined your motives and pushed through some of your fears, the next step is to sit down and decide exactly what your small group will look like. Now is a good time to purchase a notebook to dedicate to keeping notes in about your small group and your plans. It should be small enough that you can actually carry it with you over the next few weeks. You may be surprised to find that as you are sitting in the waiting room at the doctor's office an idea comes to you that you never would have thought of while at home.

You may also have a chance to talk to other people and will want to write down their ideas, phone numbers, etc. Don't be afraid to ask people questions. It can be interesting to start a conversation in a waiting room that begins with "I'm actually considering starting a support group Bible study sort of setting for people with chronic illness. Would you ever consider attending something like that?" and find out why or why not. A very successful pastor I know asked everyone from the grocery store clerk to people at the movies if they attended church, why or why not, and what would make them consider attending — before he ever even started his church.

Secondly, I recommend going down to your office supply store and purchasing a 1 ½-inch 3-ring binder. As you are going through the next few chapters and taking notes give each topic it's own page of paper so you file it in the binder later in an order that makes sense to you.

We are going to start brainstorming about things like the actual purpose of your group, who will attend, what kind of meetings you will have, how frequently they will meet, and all of the logistics. Remember during this time, there is no right or wrong answer and the decisions that you make now can always be changed or adapted later on to better meet the needs of the attendees as well as your own.

This section may seem a bit overwhelming because there are quite a lot of details to go over. However, remember that you are not expected to have all of the answers, but rather have a place that you can reference later in order to make sure that you have covered everything. I don't want you lying awake in the middle of the night before your first meeting realizing that one of the members uses a walker and you have eight stairs to get into your home on the front walk.

We will go through the logistics of preparing for this small group in this chapter, and the next chapter focuses on what your church may be looking for and what may increase or decrease the likelihood of them approving you to start a chronic illness small group. You may want to flip back and forth between this chapter and other chapters as you are planning.

So, let's get started!

Will your group be Christ-based?

This is perhaps the most important decision you will make. Since you are reading a book on starting a chronic illness small group *ministry*, the answer may seem obvious, however, you may change your mind down the road. Let me do my best to persuade you to not rule out a Chist-centered group (there are far too few!) A HopeKeepers group gives people the opportunity to openly discuss their faith, their illness, and all of the areas of their life that are affected by these two factors including relationships, marriage, finances, parenting, and careers.

There have been some leaders who start out desiring a Christian group, and soon they are inviting New Age speakers and opening it up to anything and anyone simply in the name of being able to "reach more people." Soon they are deep into healing philosophies that have nothing to do with the Gospel. God is not worried about the numbers in attendance and never wants you to compromise your beliefs.

1 Corinthians 9:22 says, "To the weak I became weak, to win the weak. I have become all things to all men so that by all possible means I might save some." It's okay to share your vulnerabilities so that others in pain know you have an authentic understanding, but don't go outside of your principles and beliefs to sway people. Don't let your zeal influence you. Remember, "[do not be] . . .ashamed of the gospel, because it is the power of God for the salvation of everyone who believe" (Romans 1:16).

Finding others who share your passion

It is important that you do not decide to go about this alone. As scripture reminds us, "So in Christ we who are many form one body, and each member belongs to all the others. We have different gifts, according to the grace given us" (Romans 12:5, 6). A co-leader and the people who attend will each help you in different ways.

Who do I know who could be
a co-leader or assistant for me?

A co-leader can significantly reduce the stress as well as the emotional and physical investment that you will make on behalf of the group.

Galatians 6:2 says, "Carry each other's burdens, and in this way you will fulfill the law of Christ." Although it may seem burdensome to have another person to consult with on all issues at first, you will find in time that having a co-leader can be a form of preventative maintenance.

You may or may not actually live with a chronic illness. One of the only requirements for official HopeKeepers groups however, is that there is a person in a leadership position who has a chronic illness. The co-leader can be someone who is simply interested in standing beside you in this venture, or he or she may be someone who is a parish nurse, a counselor, or other professional.[6]

Co-leaders can assist with anything from making phone calls to running errands, leading the group when you are unable to attend, and they can also provide feedback on how they believe the group meeting transpired. For example, she may be able to pick up on people's body language during the meeting, or speak to people afterwards as they are leaving about what they enjoyed or would like to see happen differently.

I remember when I first got married being home alone and getting frustrated over something to do with the VCR not working (remember VCRs?) In anger, at both the machine

---

[6] If a person is in a volunteer position, but they also have some kind of professional degree in the helping field, make sure to talk to your church and this individual about clear boundaries that must be made so that no one is legally at risk by what could be considered professional advice.

and my body, I finally plopped down on the carpet. The problem was, in the back of my mind I knew I couldn't get up. . . I was going to be stuck there until my husband came home. In an act of anger and defiance against my illness, I sat down anyway. But I really only sat down because I *knew* eventually, in a couple of hours, my husband would be home to help me up.

There will be times that you get frustrated about something to do with your small group. Perhaps no one comes, or ten people come and five of them don't want to have anything to do with your lesson plan, they just want to complain about the church, their families, and their doctors. When you get agitated and decide to throw up your hands and "sit down" in an act of defiance and surrender, you have the ability to do so knowing that you have someone, your co-leader, there beside you who will help you up.

You don't want to be like the person in the commercial that hollers, "I've fallen and I can't get up!" right? Way before that commercial aired, God told us that same advice: "Two are better than one, because they have a good return for their work: If one falls down, his friend can help him up. But pity the man who falls and has no one to help him up!" (Ecclesiastes 4:9, 10)

So my best advice is don't enter into starting a ministry for those with chronic illness without being sure that someone will be there to help you up when you fall down. In order to know the "secret language" of what to say and what not to say, one must have a chronic illness himself or live with a person who has a chronic illness. If you are reading this book in order to start a chronic illness ministry at your church, and you do not have a chronic condition, it is vital that someone who does live with pain or illness volunteers to co-coordinate with you. Why is this so important?

True empathy cannot be learned out of a book or manual. No matter how many books you read about illness or how many support group meetings you attend, if you do not have it, you cannot understand the emotions involved. When it comes to spiritual guidance, there are personal feelings that a leader must be in tune with in order to have an effective ministry.

And yet, sometimes no one volunteers, right? I know that I have prayed for God to provide people to fill different roles for me in my ministry and sometimes the exact right person comes along that is even more than I prayed for. Other times . . . nothing. What then?

We have many HopeKeepers leaders who have gone ahead and started a group without a co-leader, and they have found that people eventually do step into the role.

> "I couldn't find a co-facilitator, but I felt led to start it anyway. Through starting the group, now I have another gal who co-facilitates with me. If you start it and others see what you do, they would most certainly help you out when needed. They don't want the group to be cancelled when I can't make it, so someone has stepped up." –Judy

Pat Sikora, author of *Why Didn't You Warn Me? How to Deal with Challenging Small Group Leaders*, shares on her website the following about co-leaders:

> "Your co-leader should have a good mix of leadership qualities. However, they may be dormant or under-developed. Your mission, should you decide to accept it, is to identify *potential*–and then to help that potential develop into leadership.
>
> You'll want to try to select someone you feel has gifts, talents, or strengths that complement yours. . . Be aware

that since your co-leader is your counterpart, he or she may not be your best friend. In fact, you may find yourself frustrated at times with the very assets you selected the person for. It's a lot like marriage. Those aspects of your partner that best counterbalance your weaknesses will probably be the very ones that drive you crazy!"[1]

Take a few days, or even weeks, to pray about who God would bring along side you to be a helpful co-leader. Remember that this person may not actually have a chronic illness. He or she may have a spouse with an illness, a child with an illness, or perhaps they are in the helping profession and would like to apply their knowledge to your group. This person may also not be a good friend of yours. It may be someone in the church who you have admired from afar for his leadership abilities or involvement with those in the church with illness or disabilities. Or, it may be a friend of yours or even your spouse.

Whom do I know who would likely attend?

First of all, do you know people in your church body or community who would likely attend? If you do not know of anyone who has a chronic illness, but you simply assume that they are out there and they would be eager to attend, you need to start asking around and talking to people about what their needs are and if they would actually attend the group. Many people may have a chronic illness, but the likelihood that they all will want to attend your group is actually very slim.

Although you can see the benefits of a small group environment, there will be some people who will be skeptical about what will actually happen at the group because they have had poor experiences in the past with support groups or with churches. They may sit back and watch the bulletin to see when the group is meeting, and then ask around to find out what is happening there. Does the pastor show up with a bottle of oil each week? Do you have speakers who insist that everyone try acupuncture? These are the kind of things they will be looking for.

The group may meet for months before some people will actually consider attending. Other people may have lived with a chronic illness for over ten years and feel that they have never needed a support group before, so why would they attend one now?

Just because you are aware of people who live with a chronic illness, do not assume that they will all be lining up to go to the meeting. Find out who actually does have an illness, and who would be interested in finding support and encouragement from others who also live with chronic illness.

If you are keeping notes for your binder, this would be the place to take a piece of paper and make a few lists. List the names of people you know who have an illness and would definitely attend (this list should be small), a list of those you know who have illness but you are not sure if they would attend a group, and people who may not have a chronic illness but we definitely want to know about your group in order to tell others. This may be people, who are simply interested in a ministry for those with chronic illness, or it may be professionals in your church such as doctors, counselors, nurses, pastors, chaplains, etc. It may also be caregivers of those who live in illness including spouses and parents.

Formulating your mission statement & vision statement

"Mission is everything for the servant leader. The mission that God or someone in authority entrusts to the leader is the focus of every decision and action. True servant leadership begins when the leader humbles himself to carry out the mission entrusted to him rather than his personal agenda."[2]

Now is the time to start putting into words what your purpose for this group will be. You are not writing this in stone. Your mission statement and vision statement are both flexible in the planning process, something you can come back to again and again while you are reading this book and reevaluate it and change it as needed. But now is a good time to put something down on paper that you can refer to as you are going through the next steps in deciding the logistical parts of your ministry. The mission serves various purposes including giving you focus and bringing people together. This way you have something to refer to in order to determine if your decisions reflect what your mission statement actually is. Philippians 2:2 says, "Then make my joy complete by being like-minded, having the same love, being one in spirit and purpose." A mission and vision statement can make sure that everyone understands the purpose of your group.

What is the difference between a mission statement and a vision statement?
- Mission is a general statement of ministry objectives; it is philosophic.
- Vision is a specific, detailed statement of direction and uniqueness; it is strategic.[3]

In the book *The Power of Vision: Discover and Apply God's Vision for Your Life & Ministry* George Barna explains the difference between a mission and a vision:

"When we speak about vision for ministry, we are alluding to a future-based, detailed, unique perspective

on the church's calling. When we address mission for
ministry, we are speaking of our broad-based definition
of the reason for existence that undergirds everything
the church does and stands for. While vision relates to
specific actions, mission relates two general approaches
to action. . . The two are inextricably related but are
clearly distinct."[4]

You may feel as though it takes you hours to form your
statements. This is okay. They should summarize what you
would like your ministry to accomplish. And later on, as you
are making more decisions regarding your ministry, you will
find that you are able to refer back to these statements and
see if a potential activity or decision fits into your mission
statement. It will save you a great deal of time and even
heartache.

If you get stuck, just write down whatever comes to
mind about what you would like to see your group look like
and the needs you would like it to meet. Then move on to the
next section of this book. Every so often, as you are making
more decisions, come back to your mission statement or
vision statement and see if it pops out at you more clearly.

If you would like additional assistance in understanding
how to create a mission statement, you can do a search on the
Internet for "how to write a mission statement" and
hundreds of articles will provide you with tips. Don't make
this a larger task than necessary. This is simply a tool for you
to be able to use in the future to make leading your small
group easier.

You may wish to look up some of your favorite
organizations on the Internet and see what their mission
statement is.

For example, Rest Ministries' statements are:

Rest Ministries, Inc. is a non-profit Christian organization that exists to serve people who live with chronic illness or pain, and their families, by providing spiritual, emotional, relational, and practical support through a variety of programs and resources. We also seek to bring awareness and a change in action throughout churches in the US, in regard to how people who live with chronic illness or pain are served, and teach churches effective ministry tools in ministering to this population. One tool for this purpose is National Invisible Chronic Illness Awareness Week, of which we are the founders and sponsors.[5]

Joni and Friends has a vision statement and a mission statement. They are:

To accelerate Christian ministry in the disability community. (Vision Statement)

To communicate the Gospel and equip Christ-honoring churches worldwide to evangelize and disciple people affected by disabilities. (Mission Statement)[6]

Here are some examples of mission statements for Christian illness ministry small groups:

To provide a monthly Christian small group environment to encourage people who live with chronic illness or pain within oasis where they can find tools to strengthen their relationship with the Lord and friendships to provide peer support.

First Plymouth HopeKeepers shares faith and hope with people to meet the challenges of living with chronic illness or pain.

Here are a couple of tips when writing your mission statement:

Think broadly. This should be a very general statement that has room to include future interests, but it should not be a list of all the services that you intend to provide.

Get out the thesaurus and take some time to choose powerful words that are best encompass all that you do. Do you wish to enhance, encourage, empower, or equip? Notice above that Joni and friends uses the term "accelerate" rather than something vaguer such as "move forward" or "improve."[7]

Determining your group's style

Next, write down what you feel will make your group unique and determine your group's overall feeling. Will this be a group where there are frequently speakers followed by a question and answer time, and everyone leaves after a quick prayer with some information to take home with them? Or will these be a place where you open in prayer, possibly worship, share individual needs, moved into a Bible study or lesson plan, and then close with prayer and maybe even hugs?

There are many different styles of groups and there is no wrong or right style. Since you are the leader, you need to decide what it is that you are able and willing to offer. However, you may find that people who are interested in attending may not be interested in the style that you have chosen. It is then up to you to decide if you want to change to a different style in order to better meet their needs, or stick with your original plan and possibly have the group disband sooner due to lack of interest or attendance.

---

[7] You can find some excellent list of action words on the Internet, particularly on resume writing websites. A very thorough list, for example can be found at www.resume-help.org/resume_action_words.htm

Deciding the group life span

One of the first things to consider is what you would like the *life span* of the group to be. If you feel unsure that an ongoing group will keep the interest and commitment of those involved you may decide to announce that you are starting a 6-week study over the course of twelve weeks — with an ending date. At the conclusion of the class if there is still a growing interest, you may decide to shift it into a regular group meeting that does not have an ending date.

This can have benefits, because (1) you are able to see who says they are interested in coming and who actually does attend; (2) people know that there is only a certain amount of meetings that the group will have so they are more likely to make an effort to get there, rather than decide they don't really feel like going out that evening and tell themselves, "There is always next time."

Deciding the group style

Next, what will the group format be? How will the time at your meeting be filled? Do you wish to have time allotted for people to share, pray, or network? Do you plan to go through a study or will you have speakers from your community come to share their expertise? What is the preference you and your attendees have?

Here is a list of some ideas that you may want to incorporate into the style of your group:

- Prayer — will you open and close in prayer? Will you have time for individual prayer requests? What are your plans if individual prayer requests take longer than the time you allotted?
- Worship — will there be any sort of music, such as will someone bring a guitar? Will you have a CD player with a song you would like to share?

- Fellowship—will there be time committed to sharing about one another's concerns or praises?
- Bible study—will there be an actual lesson or book that the group will go through on a regular basis?
- Evangelism—will this be a group that goes out into the community and shares about their faith in Jesus in some setting?
- Education and information—will your group be a place where people can bring in information or resources about individual illnesses, treatment options, alternative medicine, or other educational type resources?
- Service—will your group serve the church or community in some way through a project such as volunteering at a local health fair or knitting blankets for children with chronic illness?
- Social activities—will the group plan to get together outside of the typical group meeting for other events?
- Other—what are some other areas of ministry you would like to see addressed in your group setting?

Deciding on your vision statement

Now take the information you have above and write out what you see as your "vision statement."

For example, the Vision Statement of Dave Dravecky's Outreach of Hope is:

> To continue the ministry of encouragement to those suffering from cancer, amputation, or serious illness and to perform that ministry with integrity and excellence.
>
> To come alongside churches and health professionals and provide resources for them and the people they serve that deal with the emotional and spiritual aspects of living with cancer, amputation, or serious illness.[7]

The vision statement is something that you will use on printed materials. It is what will go on the church's web site. It is the reason your group exists. When you go to present your ministry idea to your church leadership, this statement will be extremely helpful in communicating your purpose for the group.

John Maxwell, author of *The 21 Indispensable Qualities of the Leader* explains how a vision will help one become a better leader in four ways: (1) a vision starts within; (2) a vision draws on your history; (3) a vision meet others' needs; and (4) a vision helps you gather resources.[8]

Maxwell explains, "Vision is everything for a leader it is utterly indefensible. Why? Because vision leads the leader. It paints the target. It sparks and fuels the fire within, and draws him forward. It is also the fire lighter for others who follow the leader.[9] [A vision] goes beyond what one individual can accomplish. And if it has real value, it does more than just *include* others; it *adds value* to them. If you have a vision that doesn't serve others, it's probably too small."[10]

How to use your vision statement

The vision statement will be helpful in being able to communicate to people who are attending the group what the reason is for the group. For example, although it can be therapeutic to a certain degree to come and complain about how no one understands what it is like to live with chronic illness, the words, "vent" and "wallow" are (I should hope) not a part of your vision statement. Your group should be a place where people can be honest with one another, but your vision statement may reflect that this is a place where people find hope, encouragement and faith to sustain them through the next couple of weeks.

When someone attempts to put his own agenda into place and make the group into what he would like it to be, it can be easier to convey the message to him that it's nothing personal, but that he was made aware of the vision statement when he started attending, and you would like to stick to the plan. If the group is not meeting his needs, and he has a different idea for a group, perhaps he may want to pray about starting his own group.

It can also be helpful in avoiding conflict down the road on doctrinal conversations. For example, if one person is determined to come each week and share how she believes that God does not want anyone on earth to ever be ill, then you may be able to remind her that the group was formed for the purpose of creating friendships and encouragement and not for discussing heavy doctrinal opinions.

Any person who joins you in leadership of the group should read and sign that she agrees with the mission statement and vision statement. You should also include a copy of this in the welcome packet for new attendees.

And, to avoid conflict later on in your group, you may even want to read your vision statement out loud every other meeting or so, just as a reminder to everyone why they are there. It may prevent people from straying too far from it, and it's also a nice way to ask your group members if they feel the vision is being fulfilled or if they have any ideas for future activities. If your vision statement includes "service" for example, you may want to read your vision statement when you ask for ideas from people about what ways they would like to see the group serve others.

Determining other statements for group cohesiveness

Your statement of faith

Every church has a statement of faith. If you are going to invite people from your community into your small group that falls under your church leadership, you should make it clear what your statement of faith is. You can ask your pastors about reprinting and including it in the welcome packet for new members. This should also be something that you have in your binder that you can reference when people have questions or wish to view it.

A viewpoint on healing

There is a great deal of controversy regarding the theological issues about healing: how it takes place, when it takes place, and why. We will discuss this more in a later chapter, but it would be wise to have a viewpoint on healing in case people have questions. This is also something that you should speak to your pastoral staff about and get their approval.

Rest Ministries' viewpoint on healing is below, and it can be reprinted with permission. Just add the citation at the bottom of it.

Rest Ministries Viewpoint on Healing

- We believe that God can and *does* heal in our current day. We also believe, however, that God offers strength in our weakness and, at times, allows us to grow spiritually, although not always comfortably, by allowing the "thorns" into our lives, (2 Corinthians 12:9).

- We believe that God can heal despite our lack of faith, if it is His will, therefore, we are not able to meet a formula of "praying harder," and be guaranteed an outcome of healing (Mark 6:5,6). Illness is not necessarily a sign that we have done something wrong (John 9:3) nor that we have "hidden sin" in our lives, (John 5:14).

- We caution against worshipping "the idea of healing" rather than God, (Exodus 20:3). Although we encourage people to pray for God's healing, we also comfort them in their pain; as we believe that we are called to comfort

others in their pain, as God has comforted us in our own
(2 Corinthians 1:3-5), even when we are still living with
pain in our own lives (1 Peter 4:10).*

*Reprinted with permission of Rest Ministries,
www.restministries.com

Writing a mission statement for your personal life

Many people find it beneficial to write a mission
statement for their personal life. Most training seminars for
pastors and others in the ministry field start with this as the
first step toward understanding how to focus their time and
energy towards their priorities and values. A personal
mission statement provides a way of being accountable to
living intentionally. If you would be interested in doing this
for your own benefit, here are some tips:

Things to ask yourself as you write your personal mission statement

- Who has God shaped me to be today in my Christian
  journey?
- What "season" am I in right now? Am I excited about
  what God has planned for me? A little scared?
  Overwhelmed? Too ill to care?
- What Christian character traits does God desire to
  develop in me in the future? Do I need to stop trying
  to "do" to serve God and instead learn to surrender
  my fears over to Him?
- What experiences has God given me within the last
  year that I can use to glorify Him? God has given me
  gifts that I can still use to serve Him, despite my
  illness. What are these gifts that I didn't have or
  didn't notice before my illness? How will I practice
  faithful stewardship of the gifts God has given me?

Jesus knew His mission. "Jesus replied, 'Let us go somewhere else—to the nearby villages—so I can preach there also. That is why I have come,'" (Mark 1:38) ". . . and on this rock I will build my church, and the gates of Hades will not overcome it," (Matthew 16:18).

Isaiah 61:1–3 is also a great example of a mission statement. "The Spirit of the Lord God is upon me; because the Lord hath anointed me to preach good tidings unto the meek. . ."

Pastor Jim Priest, Pastor at Light of the Canyon U.M.C. in Anaheim Hills, CA, says, "There's absolutely no way we can ever hope to live as God intends without being deliberate and intentional about it!"

The value of writing a personal mission statement

- It forces you to think deeply about *your* life and to clarify the purpose of your life and identify what is really important to you.
- It forces you to clarify and express succinctly your deepest values and aspirations.
- It imprints your values and purposes firmly in your mind to become a part of you rather than something you thought about once.
- Integrating your personal mission statement into your weekly planning gives you a way to keep that vision constantly before you.[11]

Does it make a difference?

According to Pastor Jim Priest, author of *The Key to Living As God Intends: Have You Written Your Mission Statement* having a personal mission statement can make a significant difference in how you live your life. He shares:

The difference between intentional living with a plan—a mission—and just existing is the difference between . . .

- deciding and drifting
- being proactive and being reactive
- making your life count for something and just surviving
- glorifying God and simply getting through the day

It can be easy to have a plan in our head, but by putting it down on paper we add focus to the larger dream. We are able to fully transform our emotions into goals. And when our ministry grows and expands, the mission statement will help us prioritize where God most desires us to utilize our gifts.

Our woundedness may have given us a particular acute understanding of the extent to which we need the Lord; thus, we understand more easily the simple fact that people need the Lord, and we become His evangelists. . . Not seeking to minister to the hurts of others, out of our hurt, can cut short an intended blessing.[12]

"You gain strength, courage and confidence by every experience in which you really stop to look fear in the face. You must do the thing you think you cannot do."
Eleanor Roosevelt

"Every leader must answer two critical questions:
'Whose am I?' and 'Who am I?'
Ken Blanchard & Phil Hodges, Lead Like Jesus

"Do all the good you can, by all the means you can, in all the ways you can, in all the places you can, at all times you can, by all the means you can, as long as you can."
John Wesley

"Most of the important things in the world have been accomplished by people who have kept on trying when there seemed to be no hope at all."
Dale Carnegie

"It is vital to remember the lesson of stewardship. God owns everything. We are simply managers. You are not the real leader or shepherd of the small group under your care. You are not the center of the group. If everyone in your small group sat in a circle, closed their eyes, and then simultaneously pointed to the group leader, they should all point upward!"
Michael C. Mack
The Pocket Guide to Burnout-Free
Small Group Leadership

CHAPTER 7

Deciding the logistics of your small group

Next we are going to move into all the details about your group. Although this may seem like a lot of work at the moment, later on you will feel much more organized and when people come to you with questions, such as, "Is it okay if my husband stays for the study? The only way I can get here is if he drives me," you will immediately be able to give them an answer.

Now that you have a better understanding of chronic illness/pain ministry and what your vision is for the small group, it's time to plan some of the logistical details.

Do you have any idea what people would like? What will make a chronic illness small group successful? Although you may be imagining a room filled with people opening up and sharing, gaining strength and encouragmenet from one another, the likelihood that most have had a different experience with a support group is quite high. Keep this in mind when making your plans. Your goal may be to create a group that provides an atmosphere that will be quite different from other experiences people have had with small groups or support groups.

For example, here is one person's description of her experience with a chronic illness support group:

"I wasn't feeling very motivated to attend the meeting but I decided to go anyway. Supposedly it would be 'good for me.' The address was a hospital. I was finally able to find the building, and then had to find a place to park. It wasn't very well lit, so I was a bit nervous walking in there at 7 p.m. with few people around. I finally found the room and plopped down in a hard sticky seat utterly exhausted. A couple of people smiled at me, but they were deep in a discussion comparing botched surgeries they had been through and about how aggravating doctors can be. The leader started the group, looking frazzled and exclaiming she would much rather be home in bed than at the meeting. There didn't seem to be any agenda. She just asked how everyone was feeling and pretty soon the topic moved into everyone comparing how many pain killers they needed. Since I 'only' take 2 Vicodin a day they all said how lucky I was to not 'be in that much pain.' I was too tired to argue. At the break a woman came over and introduced herself and she seemed friendly and positive, but then I realized it was because she sold a juice supplement and she handed me her card and insisted my symptoms would diminish if tried her product. I couldn't wait to get out of there. It was one of the most depressing places I'd ever been!"

Have you had an experience that resembled something like this? I will let you in on the little secret. The above narrative is my personal experience. Yep, it all happened just like that. And this was when I decided no more support groups until I found something that made me feel *better* when I left, rather than worse.

Here one person's description of the difference between a secular support group and a Christian-based support group:

"I think it more a matter of what I don't find at HopeKeepers Groups. I don't find that I must explain why I'm ill, why I can't get well, or why I can't control my pain. I don't see a look on a face that says, 'Are you sick again?' I am not given advice as to what to do to make me well again, the name of another doctor or a new pill to take." –Betty

So, the following sections are things for you to consider so that you will feel that you are the best prepared you can be. Remember, if you flip to the back of the book you will find a checklist that you can use or photocopy for personal use.

And here is an important thing to keep in mind while making all of your decisions. This advice comes from Bill Search, author of *Simple Small Groups: A User-Friendly Guide for Small Group Leader:*

"Some groups connect like a family. A deep bond develops. Group members share hidden pain. Personal struggles. Anxieties no one else is aware of.[1] No matter how great our vision for our group, if people don't relationally connect with each other, they will exit the group. Our goal as group leaders should be to help groups form the connecting pattern as quickly as they can. "[2]

Frequency of meetings

Earlier we talked about the style of your group and what the ideal life span of your group may be. You also need to decide how frequently you would like to get together. Your group could meet weekly, bi-monthly, or monthly. You may even start out meeting quarterly, having a special speaker come every few months and then having a social event during each quarter. Consider the schedules of the participants. Would you rather have seventy percent of the members show up once per month or thirty percent twice per month?

> "The only thing that prevents me from going to church is when I am unable to drive safely, but I can usually get a ride. I have come to church vomiting (not the contagious kind of course). I have come to church in severe pain. I have found that if you are going to be sick anyway, you might as well make the most of it. After a year of bed rest, I am not crazy about staying home. I might as well be somewhere in the presence of worship than at home in bed. Sick is sick; It doesn't seem to matter to me where I am." — Jenny

If you provide a place for connecting with others and spiritual renewal, people will do their very best to come.

Membership and attendance

Who is the group for? Who will benefit? Who would be most eager to attend? These are the questions to ask yourself before starting your group. Will your membership/attendance be open or closed? Is anyone welcome at any time or are new members welcome during a certain time period designated by the group leadership? Is membership from another organization required to qualify?

For example, if your group is part of a church must participants attend the church in order to attend the group? Can guests attend the group meetings? Many people with illness may want to have a spouse, caregiver, friend, or family member attend, especially if this person is the one who provides transportation to the meeting? If you don't allow spouses, for example, you may find a bunch of husbands and wives outside sitting in their cars waiting for the meeting to be over. Would it not be more beneficial to have them included? If your answer is yes, is this okay with other members? Is it all right on specific occasions only, or on a regular basis?

Determining discussion topics and materials

Now it's time for the fun stuff: the topic selection. At your first meeting you may want to have a 15-minute brainstorm session to have people list all of the topics they would like to see discussed in the future. This has a few benefits:

- People will be interested in returning if they know that these issues will be discussed in the future.
- People will feel like they will have some input to the group and they will be aware that the leader isn't going to be "preaching" all of the time.
- Discussing frustrations and fears will probably bring a few laughs, as everyone realizes that they aren't the only one feeling these emotions.

Here is a list from one brainstorming session:

- I would like to share my concerns about my future.
- I would like to talk about my family's future with my illness.
- I need to find ways of dealing with my husband who can't acknowledge my illness.
- I need to express frustration about the relationships I have lost since I was diagnosed with an illness.
- I'd like to talk about how to cope with people who say I am not healed because of my lack of faith.
- I would like to talk about how to raise my kids while living with this illness. How do I make them understand that God isn't punishing me?
- I'd like to hear from others how they cope and how they've managed to "get this far."

- I'd like someone to cry with when the pain gets unbearable.
- I'd like to get past the "Why me?" syndrome.
- I'd like to hear about how other people's marriages are affected by their illnesses and how they keep it positive.
- I'd like to discuss how I blame God for not healing me.
- I'd like to share experiences that are uplifting.
- I'd like to talk about research and medical updates that improve all illnesses.
- I'd like to find encouragement and hope to go on — and discover where to find it in scripture.
- I'd like to discuss something that would increase my faith in God, in people, and myself; something that would keep my feet on the solid ground.
- I'd like to hear about when alternative medicines become too "new age." Where do we draw the line?
- I would like to hear how God has worked in others' lives through illness.

"Maybe if the churches had a class just for sufferers, like they have the singles class or the retired adults . . we could each bring our experiences. We've experienced pain, health care managers, spouses, children, worries, our troubles about getting around, loss and facing the inevitable 'end.' We could share our ideas and concerns with each other. Just knowing there are others who deal with these things daily can help one with coping. It's a big step toward accepting all we must accept. Also, a class could help those who can't deal with the spiritual aspects of illness, such as the 'Why me syndrome?' or blaming God for not healing them. It seems reasonable to me that we need to develop a 'place' of our own in our respective churches." — Lynette

> "I think if I was to be motivated by anything to attend a meeting it would be pure friendship and Godly love; Just a group of people who allow me to be me and no longer have to pretend. I'm tired of the mask." — Virginia

Decide on a study

As the founder of Rest Ministries, I typically recommend starting the HopeKeepers group off with a Bible study I wrote called, *When Chronic Illness Enters Your Life*. You will find that there are not very many Bible studies that specifically address chronic illness, which is why I wrote this. Using a Bible study is a great way to kick things off because it allows people to be able to open up about their illness, but also stay focused on the purpose of the group—which is to grow spiritually in the Lord, and in fellowship with one another. The Bible study is broken down into five chapters which discuss topics such as surrendering the need for control over to God, the fears we experience when diagnosed with a chronic illness, and how to re-define relationships that are affected when one has an illness.

Rest Ministries has a follow up study called *Learning to Live with Chronic Illness* and also carry other resources that are appropriate for your group. After the first one or two studies, your group may wish to select something less illness-specific, such as a study of suffering or character building. Ask your group for feedback and to bring their ideas to you.

Once you've picked the study you may wish to do the first chapter to prepare, or perhaps the entire study. There are great discussion questions. Oftentimes just one chapter can take two meetings. Don't feel like you must follow a strict schedule. The group should be about the people and not the program. Allow people the freedom to talk through topics and have plenty of time left for prayer.

Transportation to the meeting

Consider what the options may be for people who are unable to drive to the meeting. Will anyone need a ride on occasion or for every meeting? How can this need be met? It may seem simple: "Someone can just pick them up!" But you have a group of people where one person has cataracts and won't drive more than a mile from home, another person has her husband drive her and they barely make it on time due to when he gets off work. You live on the other side of town and it would add another thirty minutes onto your way there and back. And then Jessica brings up a good point:

> "There is a man in our church who really enjoyed coming to HopeKeepers, but when the guy who gave him rides stopped coming, he asked if I could take him. (He does not have a car.) I did it a couple times, but it was suggested by our pastor—to him and me—that unless my husband could be present for the ride, I should not pick him up alone, just to stay above reproach." –Jessica

Ask your pastoral staff what they would suggest and how they may be able to assist. Is there a ministry the church has that may be able to help provide transportation?

Accessibility and comfort

Next, choose your meeting place.

- Make it as conveniently located as possible. Although some people may be willing to drive over 15 miles if they hear wonderful things about the group, the closer it is to their home, the more likely they are to come.
- If you are meeting in a public location, is it a busy time with lots of traffic? What is the parking situation? Is the parking lot well lit? How many

handicapped accessible parking spots are there? Is there security, an elevator, or a cost to park? Give good directions and a map to anyone who will be attending for the first time. Add landmarks that can be seen in the dark.

- Set the room to a comfortable temperature. Don't try to freeze anyone out or turn up the heat. Usually 72-73 degrees Fahrenheit is comfortable.

  "My husband has a particular symptom that makes it difficult for him to go to most meetings—he is always 'overheated' temperature-wise, and while he doesn't expect others to freeze to accommodate him, he really cannot sit in a normal church service for long before he's sweating profusely." -Sarah

- Does the location create the atmosphere you desire? Will it intimidate members? Is it well lit? If it's in a large building, be sure to hang up signs and alert the receptionist about your group.
- Try to have chairs that are as comfortable as possible. Avoid straight back chairs or chairs that are especially low to the ground.
- Make sure bathrooms are accessible. If you are having the meeting in a home, make sure the bathroom is available without having to climb stairs. Check to make sure the toilet handle and sink faucet knobs can be easily turned on and off.
- Inform those who will be attending to avoid wearing colognes or perfumes to the meetings. Many people are sensitive to chemicals.
- Consider your emotional limitations. If you are meeting in a public location, it is easier to end on time because you need to vacate the room, versus, if you

meet at your home people may stay up to two *hours* after the group has been dismissed.

Do not meet at your home if:

- You live more than 3-4 miles from the church
- There is not enough parking
- Available parking is more than 50 feet from your front door
- You have more than 2 stairs to get into your home (Depending on who is coming, it should be wheelchair accessible.)
- There is not enough comfortable seating (don't expect people to sit on the floor)
- Your only accessible bathroom is upstairs
- You have pets that people could be allergic to

If your church does not have a place where the group can meet, and your home is not a possibility, consider asking people in your church if they would be able to volunteer their home. Some groups have a "host" who hosts the group in her home and then the leader shows up and facilitates. You can also check into meeting at a public place, like a library or a restaurant; although these places will not offer the group as much privacy.

Meeting days and times

If people have already signed up for the small group, you can call around and get a consensus of when they would like to meet. You may find, however, that everyone has a different preference and this may be more trouble than it is worth. The best option is often to pick a time, announce it, and have people RSVP so you know if the date/time will work.

There are also some great tools online if your members have internet access. One is Meet-O-Matic at www.meetomatic.com. You just type in the meeting name, select the possible dates, and then Meet-O-Matic gives you two links, one that you can forward to meeting attendees and the other, to be used to follow-up on progress. Another tool is www.whenisgood.net. Even if you have a couple members without internet access, you may want to use this program and then enter in the information for the other members yourself.

Most people prefer to meet once a month, or possibly twice. Don't have your meetings run over two hours, in fact my recommendation would be ninety minutes at the most.

Make a point to end on time. People who are in pain will not want to stay out too long, they can't sit for long, and they were probably exhausted when they arrived, so respect their time. By letting people know in advance that you will make it a priority to end the meeting on time and then allow people free time to talk afterwards, you can avoid hurt feelings, by members feeling like their conversation is being cut off.

Let the attendees know what your expectations and limits are. If you are exhausted and need to get home by a certain time, when can you follow up with people? Letting them know in advance will prevent misunderstandings, like people getting their feelings hurt because you aren't able to stay and talk for hours after each meeting.

Expenses

How do you plan to cover expenses for things like room rental, snacks, photocopies, welcome folders, etc.? Are people comfortable with a donation jar or a membership fee such as a $10 donation? Is there another way to raise funds without asking your members for the money? What is the church willing to assist you with? Is a fundraiser a possibility?

Resource table

Having a few items available for members to pick up is a nice gesture, and new members often to gravitate toward these tables when they arrive because they can browse without feeling pressured to sit and talk to someone. You may want to have brochures of local organizations, brochures of other ministries, tracts, bookmarks, flyers about local events, etc. Rest Ministries, for example, welcomes you to print out and copy materials from the web site or daily devotionals to hand out free at your meetings.

If you are looking to cheer things up, you can also add some props to your table such as a basket of fun items like buttons, note cards, or tie some balloons to the ends of the table. Some group leaders are very creative and they decorate a table each week in some small way to go along with the theme, such as everyone may get a helium filled balloon to take home the day that the Bible study is on, "When you get bad news and the wind is knocked out of you." Or pass out seed packets of flowers when you have a study on growth.

It's a good idea to have a bottle of hand sanitizer out there on the table too. Your attendees will thank you for it!

Group activities

What kinds of activities would the people in the group like to have? Many HopeKeepers groups have summer picnics, Christmas parties, outings to an event like an outdoor concert in the park or a play, It's not uncommon for groups to have a casual potluck at someone's home. Some groups check out restaurants that have new gluten-free menus.

Are family members or friends also welcome at these events? How frequently do you plan to have these? Usually group leaders will let group members share what they would like to do and go from there.

Group projects

One of the best things you can do in your group is give people the opportunity to serve others. People with illness like the chance to serve other people—not just *be* served. They have an amazing gift of understanding what is it like to suffer and are able to extend honest compassion and empathy. The gift of offering one's vulnerability and transparency may be more helpful to someone suffering than any amount of counseling could ever hope for. Being able to encourage another person also helps people in your group take the focus off of their own pain. For some, it has been decades since they had the opportunity to actually think of something other than the next doctor's appointment. And as a group, people can collectively give their talents and time to help someone, when individually they may feel unable to commit.

Brainstorm with your group about what kinds of projects they would like to do that can reach out to other people in the church or community. Some groups knit caps for premature babies at a nearby hospital. Others put together gift baskets for people who are home-bound. You may provide a holiday party for children of parents who are going through a difficult time. If your child feels comfortable with the idea, you may want to ask his or her teacher or Sunday school teacher if you do a short presentation to the class about illness or disabilities. It's always fun to use props, so get creative! Either individually or with a group of friends, visit a local nursing home or assisted care facility and just visit with the residents; call beforehand and let someone know you are coming and about your group wanting to just encourage others. Some groups volunteer to assist in an event like a fundraiser for a nonprofit illness organization.

Most people with chronic illness have a low immune system that makes them susceptible to infections. They feel they are unable to participate in some of the group or service activities. It's nice to do different things so people have a chance to contribute, and also have an ongoing ministry effort your group is involved in, such as sending encouragement cards or organizing care baskets.

Internet usage

Are your members connected to the internet? How many "sort of know how to log on" versus those who may log on to a social network like Facebook each day? You may want to consider setting up a "hub" on the internet for your group to exchange information and encourage one another between group meetings. Would they prefer something simple like just exchanging emails, or are they comfortable using a social network group like Ning.com?[8]

It's easy to set up a simple web site using free blog software online such as Word Press. This can be a great place to post your group's calendar of events, links of resources, announcements, etc. You can also share online information with your group from other organizations and web sites as well. As the leader, having a small web site can allow you to distribute information between meetings with ease. You can post items that people print out; you can post answers to questions people had at the previous meeting, you can even post links to Rest Ministries daily devotionals or other websites articles. Use RSS feeds, link to online radio programs, videos, and more. This can quickly give your group the support that they may need that you may not be able to provide on your own.

---

[8] RestMinistriesSunroom.com is a social network that uses Ning.com. You can sign up your group as a "group" at our social network for HopeKeepers groups at www.hopekeepers.ning.com

It can also decrease your expenses, since you can decrease the amount of photocopying you do and have people print out information from the website itself. You can always have some material on hand for those not on the Internet, but for many it will be more convenient for group members and less expensive for yourself.

How to announce your group

What ways will you be letting people know that your group exists or will soon be starting? Will the church include something in the bulletin? Will they add a flyer to the bulletin? Can it be announced during a service? Could you set up a table after a church service? You will find many ways to inform people about your group in the chapter on promotion, so you may want to flip to it for additional ideas as you are brainstorming about this, and find a few that you'd prefer to start with.

It can be exciting to begin to see how the group is coming together and imagine the setting, the people, the projects, and the relationships. Once you have your mission statement complete, you will be able to get creative with your group and talk about what they would imagine if there were no limits. Their response may surprise you!

While the group should be a place where people with chronic conditions can gain strength for life and new friendships, don't be afraid to add some "sparkle" to it by suggesting ways your group can take the focus off of their own pain and encourage others outside of the group. Working toward a common goal, like creating a prayer quilt for someone or going to a concert, can create a new level of friendship that would have taken much longer to develop in a cold room with folding chairs.

"So many times we say that we can't serve God because we aren't whatever is needed. We're not talented enough or smart enough or whatever. But if you are in covenant with Jesus Christ, He is responsible for covering your weaknesses, for being your strength. He will give you His abilities for your disabilities!"
Kay Arthur

"The best learning I had came from teaching."
Corrie Ten Boom

"Too many leaders act as if the sheep . . . their people . . .are there for the benefit of the shepherd, not that the shepherd has responsibility for the sheep."
Ken Blanchard

"Every problem has in it the seeds of its own solution. If you don't have any problems, you don't get any seeds."
Norman Vincent Peale

"Learn to say 'no' to the good so you can say 'yes' to the best."
John Maxwell

"To those who are open to my teaching, more understanding will be given, and they will have an abundance of knowledge. But for those who are not listening, even what little understanding they have will be taken away from them."
Matthew 13:12

CHAPTER 8

Developing group guidelines and policies

It's a funny thing about people. . . we are human. We like to know what is expected of us. When you have a child you find yourself asking things like "Did I really need to tell you *not* to color the cat with a permanent marker?" We tend to believe that at some point common sense will kick in and we will not have to be specific about certain things. If you have worked with people in any kind of situation however, you have likely found that there tend to be occasions when you have to spell things out that you would have thought most people would have considered common sense. This is all part of leading a small group.

If the last chapter could be compared to the frosting on the cake, this one may feel more like a less appealing pan-scrubbing. Few people are enthusiastic about sitting down and writing up guidelines. Rather than considering these the rules to be used in your group, however, regard them as a way of ensuring that all members have the same information about what is expected from them. Do not skip this step and try to determine your guidelines as problems arise; if you do this people will take it personally when a rule seems to be written up due to their behavior.

What group policies will your group have?

Proverbs 12:20 says, "[there is] joy for those who promote peace." Plan for peace and put down some guidelines for your group before conflicts arise.

Then take these to the pastoral staff member who will oversee your ministry and ask for guidance and approval. You don't want to hand out a 5-page booklet of rules and guidelines, nor do you want to make people feel like they will have to jump through hoops just to speak. However, you do want people to have a general understanding of the purpose of the group and the behavioral expectations you have. These should make the average attendee feel like your group is a "safe" place to share.

> "I think we all want to help in any way we can, but I think HopeKeepers is more for spiritual support and encouragement than physical and financial help. Discussing these things and drawing the lines beforehand might be to the benefit of any group." - Jessica

Here is an example of some guidelines that you can choose from and adapt for your purposes:

- Our vision statement is____.
- We are here to listen, encourage, pray for one another and develop friendships in order to more effectively live with a chronic illness.
- We will refrain from prescribing, diagnosing or giving advice. No one should be told, "You should try ____." Avoid making judgments.
- Everything shared is to be considered confidential and should not leave the room. Members should be aware that there is no guarantee of this, however, and so avoid sharing private or sensitive information that you absolutely do not want divulged to others.

- Each individual can share or decline from sharing as he or she wishes.
- Members are encouraged to share about what gives them strength and hope.
- Remember that feelings are not right or wrong, they just are. Avoid telling someone "You should not feel that way."
- Each individual will be treated with respect. When one is speaking, all should actively listen; avoid interrupting, or whispering to your neighbor.
- Members should be encouraged to use "I" statements.
- Our group's purpose is friendship and encouragement, not deep theological debate. If you have differing opinions about healing or illness speak to someone in leadership one-on-one about your concerns.
- We expect that people are in chronic pain. If you need to get up and move around at any time, you can quietly do so without concern.
- Respect the schedule and allotted time for each portion of the meeting. Although the schedule is not set in stone, members should be conscious of not speaking for large chunks of time.
- All members are welcome to share in any of the responsibilities to make the group successful. Understand that the leader also has a chronic illness and needs assistance and encouragement.
- The leader will begin and end the meeting on time. Sometimes this means asking an individual if a conversation can be continued after the meeting or later in the week. Be mindful that this is to respect everyone's physical limitations and not meant to be inconsiderate.

- The group shall not be used for any form of commercial promotion or gain. Any member who discusses a product she is selling such as "natural juice" will be given one warning and then asked to leave.
- The discussion of alternative treatments such as acupuncture, vitamin supplements, and other treatments will not be discussed except for at designated times as determined by the leader. We are here to encourage one another, not try to "get everyone to try what cured one individual."
- Please do not wear colognes due to the chemical sensitivities of some members.
- Please leave your pets at home unless they are a service animal and then let us know. Some members may have allergies.
- Although we understand the need for cell phones to be turned on, we'd prefer they be on vibrate so as to not interrupt. Please do not text message people, check your e-mail, etc. during the group time. If you must d so, please step into another room.
- If you have a cold or are starting to get sick, please don't come. We may be able to call you on speaker phone! Since everyone has an at-risk immune system, it's important that we not share germs. Hand sanitizer is available and we urge you to use it and also bring your own pens.

Policy regarding alternative treatment discussions

Alternative treatments may seem like an odd thing to have a policy on, but I have found there seems to be one person in every group who comes to the group with great enthusiasm for an alternative treatment that has worked wonders for her and she wants to make sure every person in the group tries it. She insists that if you don't try it, "then you really don't want to get well." It is not unusual for her to be a distributor of the product as well.

One of the things people like about HopeKeepers groups is that they are a refuge away from "snake oil entrepreneurs" and so I encourage you to have a general policy that makes these topics off limits. Otherwise, your meeting can quickly turn into a forty-five minute commercial for someone's opinion on a treatment or product.

On the other hand, as your group grows and members begin to trust one another and want to know more about what treatment options people in the group are trying, they may wish to discuss this. I have found that the best way to do this is to have a special meeting, such as on a Saturday morning that is separate from your regular meeting time.

Have it be a "resource exchange." This way, members who do not wish to attend can choose to opt out. You may want to allow members to bring flyers on whatever they wish to display on a resource table. If people want to share about what is working for them, set a timer and give everyone the same amount of allotted time. Make it light hearted and jokingly tell people they can talk as fast as they want.

And what do members presenting these treatment options need to agree to? That they will never mention the treatments again. In other words, they are not allowed to come to the next meeting and ask everyone if they went and tried out all that they had encouraged them to try or if they contacted the people they had been told to.

Policy regarding the exchange of personal information

Distribution of information

Do group members want their address, phone and/or emails distributed to other members as a directory or do they want it to remain private, and they can give it out to others themselves?

Phone usage

Are people comfortable with you calling them to remind them of meetings, etc.? Is there a time of day you should not call? Is it okay to leave a message? Do their family members typically give them messages?

Contacting the leader

How do you want people to contact you to receive information? For example, would you prefer in what order members tried to reach you: via the phone, web page, email, text messaging, etc? What's the fastest way for you to respond? How long will it typically take you to respond to people? Make sure you give yourself some grace and that the group members are aware of the fact that you will try to get back to them as soon as possible but that you are not able to be an emergency contact.

Policies regarding media exposure

Can you write a press release? If not, be sure to find someone who can help. Explain the logistics about your group meetings, as well as the purpose for the group. If there are certain group members who may be willing to be interviewed by a journalist at some point in the future, keep that in mind.

Videotaping & photography

It can be helpful to videotape the group meetings for people who are not able to attend so they can hear guest speakers, etc. Inform your attendees so they can choose to sit in view or out of view of the camera. Know when conversation is personal and the camera needs to be turned off. If you aren't sure how you will use the tape, have participants sign a release form. Don't post it online without permission from those who are on the tape.

Are attendees comfortable having photos for the media, for example, if a journalist wants a photo of the group for a local story? Let them know they can sign a photo release.

Policies regarding attendees with commercial intent

How will you handle people who want to attend the group with the main intention to get individuals to buy their products? Despite policies you may have set, it's likely that some people will cross the line. What is your plan of action if you discover a member soliciting other members for commercial purposes? Is the policy different if a person approaches group members during the group meeting versus if the person calls or e-mails them at their home?

Snacks

Consider what kinds of snacks will be served. Food is a big issue for many people who live with chronic illness. People have food allergies and chemical sensitivities; people are diabetic; many have had extreme weight gain or weight loss; many cannot eat sugar or refined flour. And then there are a percentage who actually have conditions like Irritable Bowel Syndrome (IBS). It may feel like all you can serve is bottled water and a few celery sticks.

Food can also make us smile, however, and can be a great way to break the ice and get people talking while they nibble on some snacks. So ask everyone to share their suggestions. People may be eager to bring a dish of their favorite sugar-free dessert or other item that they can share. But don't stop off at the grocery store and buy cupcakes and soda.

You may ask a specific person to be in charge of snacks each week—not necessarily to bring them, but to organize who is bringing them. And decide if there is any kind of fund for expenses. Someone may be eager to share her favorite new pasta salad that is gluten-free but when people ask her to bring it she is too embarrassed to admit she cannot afford the ingredients to make enough for everyone (which can be expensive for natural ingredients).

In conclusion, some chronic illness small groups work very well and others seem to have some trouble getting off of the ground. Don't feel discouraged if your group is taking time to form, just stick with it. Over time, people will come to depend on it and feel at peace knowing there is a place of refuge where they can openly discuss their illness and their spiritual journey.

During an episode of a television sitcom a young couple ran off for a couple's retreat to get to know one another better and improve their relationship. Each couple, based on earlier events in the day, was given an assignment. For some, it was to feed one another ice cream in the hot tub, but for the lead characters, it was to peel potatoes. Why? "Increased hardship creates intimacy . . ."

The HopeKeepers group at my first church was going along fine. People were getting to know one another, a few new people had joined us, and yet there was something missing. One evening a woman came to our group and shared her struggle with both her illness and her marriage and she began to cry. Suddenly our group 'jelled' and Christ's presence was felt. We put our Bible studies down and gathered around her. We prayed for her and her fears and even one another. People who hadn't prayed aloud before, suddenly felt called to participate. Christ's presence was felt in that room in a strong way."

Joni Eareckson Tada shares this about community hardship in her book *Pearls at Great Price:*

> "This sense of being together is never stronger than when you are in the trenches with a loved one battling a common enemy side by side. Stressful situations can bring us closer together. Ephesians 2:22 says, 'And in Him you too are being built together to become a dwelling in which God lives by his Spirit.'"[1]

Has your group experienced "hardship" yet? Don't be afraid of an uncomfortable moment during a group discussion or tears as someone describes what her experience or worries. Don't feel inadequate.

And if feelings are hurt and you are forced to remind people of the guidelines, although it can be difficult and awkward, it is also a way to remind your group that you will stand up for the mission of the group, and that is for it to be a safe place for everyone. Hardship does increase intimacy. Perhaps that is one of the reasons that God allows us to experience sorrow as well as joy. He knows that there are lessons and blessings in each.

"Again and again, the impossible problem is solved when we see that the problem is only a tough decision waiting to be made."
Robert H. Schuller

"Instead of continuing to focus on preventing suffering - which we simply won't be very successful at anyway - perhaps we should begin entering the suffering, participating insofar as we are able – entering the mystery and looking around for God. In other words, we need to quit feeling sorry for people who suffer and instead look up to them, learn from them, and - if they let us - join them in protest and prayer. Pity can be nearsighted and condescending; shared suffering can be dignifying and life-changing. As we look at Job's suffering and praying and worshipping, we see that he has already blazed a trail of courage and integrity for us to follow."
Eugene H. Peterson - Job - The Message

"The hands and feet of God are strengthened when the body includes someone who is suffering."
Joni Eareckson Tada

"If you believe in what you are doing, then let nothing hold you up in your work. Much of the best work of the world has been done against seeming impossibilities. The thing is to get the work done."
Dale Carnegie

CHAPTER 9

Preparing to present an illness small group to your church

As you prepare to present the idea of a small group ministry to your church, it's beneficial and calming to feel as though you know what they are looking for. This helps you be able to best prepare, as well as increase the chances of them comprehending and supporting your vision. You will find that as we go through some things to know in this chapter, you will consistently see a theme of "it depends on your church." Every church is different and no two are alike. You will find similarities between large churches and small churches, traditional churches and churches with new worship styles, but no two are the same.

Small groups are one of the most important parts of a church

According to John Townsend, Ph.D., small groups are more than just a program.

"Let's understand the importance of small groups. From a biblical and a practical standpoint, you can't overestimate what assembling on a personal level can do in people's lives. When people are safe, surrounded by a few good and growing peers, and have the right structures in place, miracles can happen, anything — including emotional breakthroughs, wisdom and courage added, clinical issues resolved, and permanent life changes and decisions made. In a word, groups provide so many of the spiritual, emotional and relational growth experiences that people need. Groups operate as a context for the Body to help heal and mature itself: 'He makes the whole body fit together perfectly. As each part does its own special work, it helps the other parts grow, so that the whole body is healthy and growing and full of love (Ephesians 4:16, NLT).' You'd be hard pressed to find a better way to follow all of the 'one another' passages in the New Testament of how we are to treat each other: accepting, building up, being kind, admonishing and so forth."[1]

How small groups can meet a need for the ill or disabled

In the book *Parish Nursing: A Handbook for the New Millennium* the author says, "From a theological perspective, those in situations of pain, suffering, and disability will look to caring communities of faith to find meaning and purpose in their suffering."[2]

So my question is this: when they come to your church, what will they find? Will a chronically ill or disabled person find anything that acknowledges their situation in life or practical needs other than a few disabled parking spots or a bar to grasp in the restroom?

Preparing your spirit for the church's response

As you read through this book and envision what God could do to work through the experience of your illness, allow God to lead you, and when you start to wonder if you are getting in over your head, give yourself the same grace that He has given you.

God can use the defining experiences you have had living with your illness (the good and the bad) for His glory.

Also keep in mind that if your ideas are met with resistance or reluctance, this has been predicted by many of the experts in the field, including Harold G. Koenig, M.D.

> "What bothers me is that many parish nurses today have to go to great lengths to convince ministers, church board, and congregations that having a health ministry is a worthy endeavor. Even when a parish nurse offers to volunteer for such a task, she or he often meets with resistance. However, given the demographic and economic trends . . . I am absolutely certain that parish nurses in future years will no longer have to beg their congregations to play a role in this area. As churches overflowed with those who are sick, disabled, and chronically ill (and with the young families trying to care for the health needs of aging loved ones), I think all of this will change. Churches and congregations will be begging parish nurses to start health ministries to ease the burden on clergy that the huge demand for health care will create. Indeed, throughout history, it was the church that came to the rescue of people experiencing poverty, sickness, and suffering. If the church does not assume this role again in the years ahead, I believe such a lack of response will foretell a decline in the role of the church in modern society."[3]

Understanding your church's priorities

What is the key to understanding your church? Look around and see what kinds of ministries they value.

- What kinds of ministries do they feature or announce in the weekly bulletin?
- Which ministries does a pastor or coordinator share about from the pulpit?
- What ministries have banner graphics on the church's web site?

- What ministries are allowed to show a video clip of a recent event during church?
- What ministries does the church invest in financially, by bringing in speakers or providing resources for free of charge?
- What events or ministries do they accomplish every year, no matter what?
- What events or ministries have they recently begun or featured that surprised you?
- What positions have they recently filled, created, or asked for additional volunteers?
- When your church purchases ad space for the local paper, radio, or television, what are they advertising? The church service in general, an event, or a ministry such as the youth group?
- Why do people say they come to your church? For the music, the sermons, the youth program, the children's program.

Author Randy Christian shares that when a member of his church was talking to a friend at work about the church she attended her friend replied "Oh, you go to the support group church!" He says, "When she told me about this episode, I thought, *that's not a bad way to be seen.* People in our community view us as champions of the cause of the weak and needy, an image that well fits the Church of Jesus Christ."[4]

Most churches have a purpose statement and some kind of annual report or plan of intent. Wise pastors understand that as much as they would like to be all things to all people they are unable to do so and their church is not able to meet the needs of all people. Those who try to do so will fail to do all or some of the ministry well and people will fall through the cracks.

Understanding your church's style

By looking at what ministries within your church currently receive the most support, you may save yourself some heartache later. For example, you will find some churches prioritize outreach and they are frequently organizing activities or events that reach out to the people in the community by offering services, often free of charge. Other churches that are perhaps more traditional want people to first come to church, then become a member of the denomination, and then attend the extra functions and events.

If you would like your illness ministry to be one that reaches out to those in the community, you will find an outreach-oriented church (such as a Willow Creek style or non-denominational) much more receptive to the idea than a traditional church. "Anyone who has tried to make change in a church or business knows the explosion that can occur when a new plan is poured into old ways of doing things." [5]

If we have a small group, what area of the church will a HopeKeepers ministry fall under?

You will discover that the place where your illness/pain small group ministry will be delegated to depends largely on the church. Ministries for those who live with chronic illness or pain have been known to be designated to the following areas of ministry: small groups, women's ministry, congregational care, hospital visitations, chaplaincy, Stephen ministries, parish nursing, pastor's personal ministry, support groups, care groups, home fellowship, counseling, grief recovery, crisis care, and even hospice care.

One of the first steps toward presenting a chronic illness ministry to your church is to decide where it may best be accepted. The questions to ask are:

- Who currently oversees a ministry where he or she is well aware of the need for more fellowship, outreach or follow up for those living with daily physical pain?
- Who do I know personally who is active in church leadership who has a chronic illness or has an immediate family member who has an illness?
- If you don't know anyone personally, ask a few close friends who are active in Sunday School class, the women's ministry, or other areas of the church, if they know of someone in leadership who would be receptive to an illness ministry.

Then, this person may be the best individual to approach with your vision and see where she may direct you. As you are well aware, those who have personally experienced illness or pain in their immediate family are most receptive to understanding why the current service the church offers may not fully be meeting the needs.

Once you have found a church leadership member who will be your advocate, ask how you should go about presenting your idea for a small group to the church. Depending on the church there may be a formal meeting where you go in and present the idea to the leadership team with an oral presentation. Or you may just turn in some paperwork that is your vision statement for your ministry. In some cases, you may have a personal meeting with one or two people and talk about what you would like to see happen in the church in regard to your vision and passion.

What is a reasonable expectation for support?

Connie Kennemer, a founding member of Moms in Touch International says about the HopeKeepers Start up Kit: "It's hard to construct a building with an empty tool chest! The HopeKeepers Start Up Kit is beautifully filled with wonderful tools to help build a church, a small group, or personal ministry to the chronically ill." A start up kit is not a necessary purchase, just a convenience, but you must decide what tools and resources you need to give your ministry the best chance.

What books are necessary for you to feel well prepared? Do you need a budget to photocopy some articles for welcome folders? Are there funds that can purchase Bible studies for the people who cannot afford them (Usually, people who attend small groups can afford $5-10 for a book, but the people who are attending an illness group may be on a very limited budget, and possibly on disability assistance, and they simply do not even have an extra $5).

Sadly, some churches do expect that a new ministry should be built without the investment of any tools. But would you try to build a building without both a hammer and a level?

If you are asking your church to assist you in purchasing materials in the $50 to $300 range to start a new ministry you should not feel like this is impractical. Wise ministry leaders understand that there are costs involved and expect to have an outline of a budget so they know what the funds will cover and what the expected expenses down the road will be. In his book, *Leading Life-Changing Small Groups,* author Phil Donahue offers this piece of experience to church leadership:

> "We have found it worth the investment to allocate significant resources to the training, development, and growth of group life throughout the church. Be

prepared to change your budget, staffing, and support systems to make small groups productive."[6]

If the church decides that they will *not* invest even $50 for the basics, this should be a red flag for you. Be aware that if they are not able to invest in it financially, they likely will not announce your ministry in the bulletin, provide transportation to your members, or meet other needs you may expect. Churches are not any different than individuals when it comes to applying the scripture Matthew 6:21: "For where your treasure is, there your heart will be also."

You should not be expected to build a successful ministry without even a toolbox. If you get this response from your church, know that it is not a personal issue or your fault. Rather, it may just not be a match between your ministry ideas and the church's mission.

Again, let me emphasize that just because your church says, "No, we don't have any budget for you," does not mean they are an uncaring church or that the church is led by uncompassionate, heartless people. *No* church can be all things to all people, and there is only so much money and volunteer hours available to support all the ministries. No church can allow a ministry to be birthed from every person who determines they have found a need and a calling or every church would be filled with hundreds of small ministries—none of them truly effective

But. . . I think it's important for you to have reasonable expectations of what your church may or may not provide for you. The leadership of the church should not necessarily "lead you on" by agreeing to allow you to start the ministry, and then leave you flailing in six months, unable meet the needs you have discovered.

What will the church want to know?

Although each church will be unique in what they may ask you about starting a support group environment/Bible study/small group, there are many things that every church leadership team will want to know before approving the group. Sit down with a piece of paper and this list of questions and answer them or seek out the answer so you feel better prepared for their questions.

- What will be the purpose of this group?
- Why do you specifically feel called to lead this group?
- Tell me your testimony
- Who will attend this group? (Men? Women? Does age matter?) What about those with canceer?
- Where will the group meet?
- How frequently will the group meet?
- What materials will you be using?
- Where will you find leadership support?
- Who is Rest Ministries/HopeKeepers and what is their statement of faith? Where does their funding come from?[9]
- What is your budget or estimated expenses for this group for the next six months? For the next two years?
- How do you plan to let people know that this group exists?
- Is this a group for members of the church only or community members too?
- What kinds of illness do people need to have to qualify?
- Can people who are not chronically ill attend? What about caregivers or spouses?

---

[9] See more at restministries.com

- Have you led a small group before?
- Have you been through our church's small group training? [Many churches have special leadership training]
- Will you have a co-leader?
- Who will lead the group when you are too ill to attend?
- What area of ministry do you see this falling under at the church?
- What other needs do you see your group having where the church should respond?

Now that you have some of the basic answers for the church about your vision, let's look more closely at some questions they may ask you that can be considered more difficult than the logistical questions.

"You may think, who am I that anyone should listen to me? Why should anyone care what I have to say? Don't fool yourself. In Christ, you're completely competent. Second Corinthians 13:4 reminds you, 'For to be sure, He was crucified in weakness, yet He lives by God's power. Likewise, we are weak in Him, yet by God's power we will live with Him to serve you.' It is by God's power I serve the Lord. And it is by His power—and His power only—you can serve too."
Joni Eareckson Tada, Pearls of Great Price

"For a long time it had seemed to me that life was about to begin—real life. But there are always some obstacles in the way, something to be gotten through first, some unfinished business, time still to be served, a debt to be paid. Then life would begin. At last it dawned on me that these obstacles were my life."
Alfred D. Souza

"There is always the danger that we may just do the work for the sake of the work. This is where the respect and the love and the devotion come in–that we do it to God, to Christ, and that's why we try to do it as beautifully as possible."
Mother Teresa

"Surrender your soul, center your thoughts, ask the Spirit for help, weigh your words. Then pray with joy and certainty that God will take those words to accomplish His grand and glorious purpose!"
Joni Eareckson Tada, Pearls of Great Price

CHAPTER 10

Questions and concerns your church may have

Your church, like many, may already believe that they have an illness ministry. Many churches believe if they have someone who delivers casseroles and someone who prays for the chronically ill to be healed then the chronically ill are "covered."

They may be concerned about giving responsibility of a brand new ministry to someone who is chronically ill. Some people will not see your illness as an asset, but rather as a liability.

As you are talking to your pastor about the excitement you feel in starting such a group, he may be wondering who is going to lead the group when you are too ill to get out of bed or unable to drive. He may wonder if you understand how deep the emotional needs may be of those who are ill. He's wondering if this group is just for those with physical illness, or mental illness too. And what about all those depressed people who may want to call you in the middle of the night?

Sometimes the pastor or leader in the church has had a personal experience with illness himself or with his own family and can quickly see the benefits such a ministry would have provided him. Other times, a pastor may see this new ministry as only one more headache.

If his response is the later of the two, take a moment to give him the benefit of the doubt and understand where he may be coming from. I recently read the quote, "Where two or three are gathered in His name . . . there will be problems." It is sad but true, and since we are all sinners, we will always be imperfect people. Pastors have a lot to deal with every day.

And, admit it. Don't those of us with a chronic illness have a little bit of baggage (myself included!)?

We have limitations in our abilities of being able to commit to certain things simply because our disease is unpredictable.

We may be in a place spiritually where we are feeling ready to share, and yet we are still in place of spiritual growth where the pastor may feel that we are not yet ready to be put in charge of others who are spiritually fragile.

We may seem emotionally grounded one day and flying off the handle a week later because of a new medication that has made us grumpier than we've ever experienced. But new medications don't let us off the hook. Oswald Chambers, author *of My Utmost for His Highest* says, "We all know people who have been made much meaner and more irritable and more intolerable to live with by suffering: it is not right to say that all suffering perfects. It only perfects one type of person . . . the one who accepts the call of God in Christ Jesus."

In this chapter, I would like to share some of the questions that your church leadership may ask to you when you bring your ideas and proposal to them, so that you can feel as well-equipped as possible. In fact, while you are preparing a proposal to take to your church, you may want to address some of these concerns head on before they even have a chance to communicate them, so they know you are aware of them.

147

Don't forget to spend time in prayer while you are preparing. This may seem like common sense, but so often we can get caught up in the excitement of the ministry that our time with the Lord shrinks—I know because I am guilty of doing this. When your excuse is to delay your quiet time because you have phone calls to make and flyers to distribute, it's time to regroup and look at your real motives. Remember to keep your time fellowshipping with the Lord your first priority.

We'd really prefer you to be healed first

I understand that you may be overflowing with the desire to be able to talk to someone else about what God is teaching you through this experience. And you may also be reflecting on your emotional journey, distinctly remembering moments of loneliness, frustration, and sadness. Perhaps you just want to be able to offer your friendship and understanding to even just one person who is on this same journey, so he or she does not have to travel it alone.

It can be devastating to hear the words, "This sounds good. You should go and pray for healing and get your illness all sorted out and then come back and we'll talk."

Yes, pastors have said this.

I have seen many people go to the church leadership team and express a desire to start a chronic illness small group only to be told they needed to first be physically healed. While a person who leads an alcohol recovery class does need to be in recovery, the person who leads a chronic illness small group does *not* have to be physically healed in order to be an effective leader. But this theology depends on your church. You may want to ask your pastor if this is a general attitude, or truly a theological policy the church has.

There is no formula that can predict if your ministry idea will be seen as something necessary and that will meet a need, or one more ministry that will burn out and leave people feeling abandoned and frustrated with the church.

The chronically ill people we know could never be dependable enough to lead a group

Their concerns are valid. In fact, many people have not experienced a "healthy" relationship with a chronically ill friend. The people they know who are ill may be living a life with the four "Ds" - discouragement, debt, depression and draining! In his book, *Chronic Fatigue Syndrome, Christianity, and Culture* James M. Rotholz shares what it can be like to be a person who lives with CFIDS, also known as chronic fatigue immune-deficiency syndrome. This is the type of person many people have come into contact with who live with illness and they cannot imagine someone like this leading others.

> "The disability of CFIDS brings out all that is nasty and negative in one's personality. The illness has a way of making it all but impossible to express those qualities that are admirable in one's self. There is a direct relationship between the way one feels (happy, sad, sick, tortured) and the way one relates to others. In that PWC [people with CFIDS] feel sick so much of the time, it only stands to reason that their interactions with others are often characterized by irritability, frustration, and short-sightedness."[1]

Why have most people only had experiences with the chronically ill who may be irritable? Because it's likely that those who were ill and not so irritable, either didn't share about their (likely invisible) illness, or the people did share, but since it did not meet the expectations of what an ill person would act like it went right over the head of the person listening.

For example, Susan may have shared with her women's Bible study leader, Beth, last year that she had been diagnosed with diabetes, but since then, she has looked fine. Beth has no idea that Susan has been seeing multiple doctors, in and out of the hospital for a foot infection, and trying to find the right insulin level. Diabetes has tried to take over Susan's life, but Susan has fought back and done everything to keep moving forward and not make a big deal out of her illness with her friends. In fact, since she has been doing her best to lose weight, she really didn't want them all to know about the diabetes. When her sisters heard about it, they just told her that it was her own fault since she had been forty pounds overweight most of her life. Susan couldn't bear to have her Bible study friends give their opinion on why she had become diabetic. Most of them don't even know.'

Statistics your church may find of interest

The best way to speak to your church about your desire to begin a HopeKeepers group is from your heart. You have lived with illness and pain and you know that despite your faith, life can become difficult. We have provided some interesting thoughts, however, that may fit in well with your presentation.

- Nearly 1 in 2 people in the United States (over 133 million) live with chronic illness.[2] Most times illness is invisible. Although your church may believe that HopeKeepers would only apply to a small group of people in the church, in fact, over one-third of the church would be eligible participants. If you include the person's spouse, this number grows even more.

- A study discovered that 49% of women diagnosed with breast cancer became "more religious." Very few churches have an active group for people who live with illness or pain, although people are searching for it.[3]
- Despite their good intentions, churches have not yet learned how to effectively reach out to the chronically ill. *Philip Yancey, author of Where is God When it Hurts?* addresses the church and physical pain by saying, "The church often responds with more confusion than comfort."
- Attending church is vital to both the physical and emotional health of individuals. Studies have shown that the more often one attends church, the more likely one will have a healthier life. Similarly, the stronger one's faith, the more likely one will follow doctor's orders and have a quicker recovery from acute medical conditions. When a person is facing physical chronic conditions, one often reaches out to others for support. Statistically, the more frequently one attends church, the larger the support network becomes. In fact, a study showed that frequent church attenders had a social support three times as large as non-attenders.[4]
- One study of 850 men hospitalized for acute illness found that those who used their religious faith to cope were significantly less depressed, even when taking into account how severe their physical illness. In fact, the clinical effects of religious coping showed the strongest benefit among those with severe physical disability. Some 87 patients hospitalized with serious illness who also then suffered depression were followed over time in another study. The patients with a deep, internalized faith recovered faster from the depression, even when their physical condition wasn't improving.[5]

- Despite what we may assume, 60% of those who live with daily illness or pain are between the ages of 18 and 64. According the USA's National Health Interview Survey in 1994, out of 50,000 households, 20.7 percent of the disabled adults polled were divorced or separated, compared to 13.1 percent of those without disabilities. Depression is 15-20% higher for the chronically ill than for the average person. However, the significance of one's faith has shown to lower one's risk of depressive symptoms and aid one in better handling a stressful medical event. Various studies have reported that physical illness or uncontrollable physical pain are major factors in up to 70% of suicides; and more than 50% of these suicidal patients were under 35 years of age.[6]

- New national survey data show that more than one-fourth (26%) of U.S. adults who seek pastoral care have disabilities. The percent with disabilities among seekers of pastoral care increases with age and is higher among women. Among women over 65 years of age, more than one-half (52.4%) of pastoral care seekers have disabilities. These rates of disability are much higher than those in the general population, among whom only 14.7% of adults have a disability.[7]

- People with disabilities are much less likely to attend religious services at least once per month when compared to people without disabilities. However, more than 8 out of 10 people with and without disabilities consider their faith to be important to them. Therefore, something else – likely a barrier of architecture or attitude – is holding people with disabilities back from attending services. Disability is defined as "has a disability or health problem that prevents him or her from participating fully in work, school, or other activities."[8]

- 47% of Americans with disabilities attend religious services at least once per month, compared to 65% of those without disabilities. Most congregations work hard to be hospitable and welcoming, but the barriers which exclude children and adults with disabilities from full participation may not be easily understood or identified. Certainly, it is easier to add ramps, pew cuts, accessible parking places and restrooms than to remove the barriers of limiting attitudes and stereotypical thinking.[9]

There are not that many people in our church who have a chronic illness

They may ask, "Is there really a need for this kind of ministry at my church? Are people calling the office to see if we have a small group ministry for those with illness or pain?" Do people come forward at your service and ask for prayer when they have been diagnosed with an illness? Yes, they likely do. "But they ask for healing" your pastor replies. "Not to get together with other people and talk about it."

Despite the fact that over 133 million people are living with chronic illness, we don't seem to notice them. We don't see their pain. Why is this?

> "I used to go to church all of the time. It gradually became hard to sit through the service. My legs would get stiff, and so I couldn't just stand up and walk out gracefully and quietly. So I missed a few weeks and no one seemed to notice. Eventually, I just quit going. I try to have a quiet time now and then and I still believe in God and all of that, but my relationship with God has really faltered. I just felt like none of those people at my church really understood, and they were my last hope."
> —Sarah

Regardless of what we may see, there are *many* people who live with invisible chronic illness who are attending your church right now. If you could take your church, turn it upside down, and shake it so all of the people who live with invisible chronic illness fell out, you would lose entire pews . . . maybe half the choir. Don't be surprised if your pastor and a handful of children are included.

> "One of the hardest things for me is that I do not look disabled at all. I have a terminal illness, but my body appears healthy from the outside at this stage of my disease. People cannot see anemia when you wear make-up. They cannot see my malignant hypertension. They do not know I have had four major surgeries on my head. They just say, 'Oh, what lovely blond hair you have!'" —Jenny

We already have a ministry for those with illness

Many churches genuine believe that they already are meeting all of the needs people who live with a chronic illness or pain may have. Quite frequently however, these ministries revolve around meals, visitations, and perhaps transportation. There is rarely an actual small group environment where people who live with illness can fellowship with others who live with illness.

Historically, churches have done a wonderful job at responding to the needs individuals have within the church body who have an acute, short-term health crises and who need assistance with things like meals, get well cards, transportation, and childcare.

I remember overhearing one of my pastors once say, in regard to his wife becoming chronically ill, "It has been wonderful! We get free meals! A group of women came over and cleaned the entire house. Someone even did my ironing this week. Even my wife never did my ironing." I can hope that he was joking around and trying to find humor in what was a very difficult situation; but quite honestly, there was a little part of him I believe that actually found the response from the church to be a nice perk of not only his job, but also of his wife's illness. (And I can imagine that his wife would not have been quite so thrilled about her new chronic illness giving her the privilege of having people in her home doing her husband's ironing.)

Let me give you an example of how a person with a chronic illness may view the church's current ministry that the church insists covers the needs of those who live with chronic illness.

> Mary lives with lupus and has very little energy as well as severe flares, resulting in being bedridden some of the time and being in a great deal of pain the rest of the time. She has had to give up a great deal, including going to many of her children's soccer games because she can only be outside in the sun a very limited time, even with long sleeves, sunscreen and shade. She recently has begun to lose her hair, and although she has started a new medication, it makes her feel quite ill most of the time and her body continues to have all the aches and pains associated with what they are now saying is fibromyalgia.

> But on Saturday nights she goes to bed early and tries to get some rest, she gets up on Sunday and puts on some makeup and perhaps a wig, and she drives herself to church and puts on a smile. She may go home and spend the rest of the weekend in bed, perhaps even into Monday. Her husband gets up on Monday morning and gets the children off to school and she tries to get as much rest as she can before the kids come home so that

she can prepare dinner and help them with their homework.

When she finally gets up Monday afternoon and looks outside, she sees that her neighbor, who also goes to the church, has people dropping off meals and picking up her children to care for them for a few hours, since her neighbor is currently undergoing chemotherapy for breast cancer. There is no way in the world that she would want to deny her neighbor this gift of compassion and help from the church. And yet, at the same time, she may feel a sense of frustration and even resentment that no one in her church seems to understand that it takes everything in her to function each day and try to provide her family with a sense of security and care too.

People who have a chronic illness will likely have seasons of needs throughout the rest of their lives. There may be a season of a few months where transportation and meals are a real necessity. And then this person may not need other practical assistance until the next year. On the other hand, someone with a chronic illness may not need *significant* assistance, but they need *consistent* assistance.

For example, morning can be very difficult for people who have autoimmune diseases because their body has not yet "kicked in" and started functioning well until noon. Although they may be able to take their kids places later on in the day, they are not able to drive in the mornings and one of the things they desire the most is for their children to go to Sunday School class. Having a volunteer who is able to pick up the children on a weekly basis and make sure they go to Sunday school may be a practical gift that your church can help provide that would not strain the church's resources or even need a line in the budget.

We all have a cross to bear. Do the chronically ill really need their own ministry?

Chronic illness and disability are often not seen as their own entity of suffering. Although our Christian bookstores now have shelves stocked full of books on life's problems that we may encounter, chronic illness is simply seen as a form of suffering, and therefore, is often seen as something that does not need to be specifically addressed. Since the Middle Ages, Christianity has viewed impairments or physical ailments as indistinguishable from other forms of suffering. Susan Reynolds Whyte, author of *Disability Between Discourse and Experience*[10], writes "Infirmity [impairment] and poverty were part of God's varied creation—the order of things. The response to difference was charity, spirituality, and morality."

There are many excellent books written by Christians on the topic of suffering, and a chronically ill person will likely find some comfort in them. We all wish to be able to identify, however, with the specific circumstances. Sometimes we need illness to be addressed specifically, especially since it brings out so much confusion with regard to faith and spirituality. Who among us would not enjoy picking up a book that described what we are feeling and gave us the sense that we are not alone in our struggles?

> "I got your newsletter and sat down on the couch to read it right away. As soon as I started to read the front page, I started to cry because you explained exactly how I had been feeling the last week, but had been unable to express. I felt such a sense of relief knowing I wasn't alone. My husband walked in and saw my tears and said, 'What's wrong?' and then I had him read it too and he cried with me. Thank you for this gift." -a subscriber of . . .*And He Will Give You* Rest newsletter, a former publication of Rest Ministries, Inc.

157

None of us like to feel that we are alone in our experience. Discarding the pain and the emotional and spiritual upheaval that illness brings into our life as merely "suffering" is not acceptable. We are aware that life is not going to be easy. We are warned in 1 Peter 4:12 "Do not be surprised at the painful trial you are suffering, as though something strange were happening to you," but we still want someone there beside us.

Isn't this what a pastor is for?

Surprisingly, most pastors do not receive specific training for chronic illness or disability ministry. Many of them will come to understand what to say and how to respond out of their experience. You may ask, "If the pastor isn't even addressing this issue, does it really need to be addressed?" The answer is, of course, yes. "Religion serves ordinary people who have accidents and diseases, who bear children with congenital conditions and develop heart problems, arthritis, and much more in maturity," says Blair and Blair, authors of *Pastoral Counselors/Religious Professionals and People with Disabilities*[11]. "Life is change, not always for the better. And very often the parish minister will be the spiritual helper to whom people will turn."

When people are diagnosed with a chronic illness, it affects their entire being, especially their spirituality. Even the person who may claim to be an atheist is suddenly asking, "Why me, God?" When a person is diagnosed with a permanent disability or a chronic illness, many well-meaning pastors are at a loss as to how to explain why the person is going through what he or she is coping with. The person is dealing with a wide array of emotions.

Blair and Blair state "This is the time of greatest need, as well as a time when spiritual and physical suffering coexist in its rawest form. People have their spiritual advisors label them as sinners, question their faith, chastise them for feeling angry, tell them they were 'chosen by God' to be 'an inspiration,' and avoid any discussion of the dramatic life changes these people and their families are facing."[12]

> "On a Sunday morning I read an article about a group meeting for chronic pain sufferers. I had never been to any group meetings before but knew I had hit bottom with pain and depression. From the very first meeting I had a feeling of happiness and serenity that I had not had in as long as I could remember. You know you can share anything, your fears, and frustration and not feel judged. I guess one of the most important things I have come away with is closeness with God, with friends, and knowing there is always hope." -Judy

"Support for people with disabilities and their families can mean the survival of the family unit, and the most effective religious professionals know what support is needed and where to find it," writes Blair and Blair. "It is not unusual for families to consult a minister for advice about counseling, effective support groups, shared care programs, and sources of economic aid."

But all of us need relationships. People who live with daily physical pain are likely to feel isolated, even when surrounded by loved ones or pastoral staff. "No one knows what I am going through. No one understands!" is often said in frustration. Fortunately, a small group ministry can help take these feelings of loneliness and isolation away, as people are given the opportunity to socialize and grow with other Christians who also face the "thorn of illness."

Can't they just go to a secular support group?

They could just go to a regular support group, such as a group organized though the local hospital or illness organization. However, even these groups have their drawbacks.

> "The support group for fibromyalgia patients [Jenni] joined shortly after her diagnosis increased her sense of frustration. It was filled with people years older who told her things like, 'You're too young to be sick' or 'It can't be *that* bad, you're so young!" Despite the fact that many autoimmune disorders and chronic illnesses emerge during childbearing years, such attitudes about illness and age are not uncommon, and they make this journey more complicated. It also compounds the isolating nature of illness—not only are you sidetracked from the majority of your healthy peers by illness, but you're further marginalized from the very patient group you can finally claim as your own."[13]

However, for many people this does not truly meet the needs that they have, especially their spiritual needs. If they are truly to search out and find what will get them through this suffering, should not we encourage them that it will be a relationship with Christ that can be their foundation for the peace that passes understanding?

What is it like to live with a chronic illness or disability? Here is one author's raw depiction:

> ". . . the kind of mundane suffering that many disabled Americans face is in a way more difficult to bear [than other forms of suffering]. It is the day-in and day-out, unrelenting pain that serious illness and disability often inflict. This kind of suffering requires more than a moment's grit and grace. It requires a sustained battle against a ubiquitous foe, and all too often within the

context of ridicule. Even a low level of sustained pain and suffering can be so insidious that, barring God's constant intervention, sooner or later even the most iron will and noble spirit must break. The concept of 'Chinese water torture' is based on this understanding of the complex nature of the human psyche."[14]

Do we truly want to leave the person suffering in this way to be encouraged and counseled by people who believe that perhaps there is no God. . . or maybe there are many Gods?

"On a Sunday morning [at church] I read an article about a group meeting for chronic pain sufferers. I had never been to any group meetings before, but knew I had hit bottom with pain and depression. From the very first meeting I had a feeling of happiness and serenity that I had not had in as long as I could remember. You know you can share anything, your fears and frustration, and not feel judged. I guess one of the most important things I have come away with is closeness with God, with friends, and knowing there is always hope." —Judy

There is no doubt that support groups are beneficial. Stanford Medical School researchers recently found that women with metastatic breast cancer[10] survived longer if they were part of a support group led by a psychiatrist or social worker along with a therapist who had breast cancer in remission. Five years after the study began, the data showed that women who became part of a support group lived twice as long as the women who did not participate, which surprised the study's lead scientist, David Spiegel, who had

---

10 Cancer that had spread to other organs or bones

set out to *disprove* the idea that psychosocial interventions could prolong life. (4)

This said, support groups don't meet all of our needs. Whether a person is seeking to express his anger at God or seeking for the support of God, he is oftentimes discouraged from expressing these thoughts at secular group meetings. It is common to leave the meetings feeling as though something is missing. Oftentimes, these meetings focus on the education of one's illness and how to live a productive life despite the limitations. Good facilitators present positive agendas for the meetings, but ultimately, the only hope that is given is hope for a cure or a more effective drug.

Although a cure or more effective drug would be nice, as Christians we don't need to put our ultimate hope in these things, because we have hope in God. Our hope lies in things unseen. Hebrews 11: 1 says "Faith is being sure of what we hope for and certain of what we do not see." When a faith-centered support group meets, we can always leave with a hope that is not of this world; a hope that regardless of what lies ahead in the medical world, we have a better world that we will one day be a part of: heaven. Our hope can be our anchor for our soul, firm and secure and hope will not be cut off, (Proverbs 23:18).

> "I need a place to talk about the spiritual aspect of living with a chronic illness; a group of people who are a refuge; people who understand what it's like to deal with pain every day. I feel that the spiritual journey one takes when she is diagnosed with a chronic illness is an important part of how she copes and lives out her life."
> —Patti

Friendships with other Christians who are experiencing similar challenges, frustrations, and even lessons are a vital part of one's emotional well-being. Though "even in laughter the heart may ache," (Proverbs 14:12b), most of us who live with chronic illness or pain will agree that there is nothing that can replace friendships with other Christians who understand our journey.

"The times we find ourselves having to wait on others may be the perfect opportunities to train ourselves to wait on the Lord."
Joni Eareckson Tada

"What would happen if you believed it, if you came to the place where you knew it was true? Your life would never be the same... If we believed that... we could do anything. We would follow him anywhere!"
John Eldredge, Waking the Dead

"A leader takes people where they want to go. A great leader takes people where they don't necessarily want to go but ought to be."
Rosalynn Carter

"The most important thing in communication is to hear what isn't being said."
Peter F. Drucker

"Does your life ever seem fragmented, random, and without real direction or meaning? That's a lie of the enemy! You truly are a part of God's grace story, and every day of your life—whether you realize it or feel like it or not—it's weighted with kingdom purpose, eternal significance, and high destiny. You have a role to play today as you walk in His will and speak of His love and salvation to those who cross your path."
Joni Eareckson Tada, Pearls of Great Price

CHAPTER 11

Sharing your vision with the church

According to Ken Blanchard, author of *Lead Like Jesus*, "The journey of servant leadership starts in the heart with motivation and intent. Then it must travel through the head, which is the leader's belief system and perspective on the role of the leader."[1] In this chapter we will talk about putting together your motivation for starting a group (your testimony will fit in here), your intent, and your belief system. And then we will move on to come to ascertain the best way to communicate your message to your church leadership.

Preparing to share your testimony

Your testimony is your story about how Christ has made a difference in your life. In the Bible, the apostle Peter tells us that we were chosen by God "to do His work and speak out for Him, to tell others of the night-and-day difference He made for you." (1 Peter 2:9, *The Message*)

Your testimony is personal and unique and no one can argue with it. God has given each person a distinct set of experiences that are precious to Him. As a teenager, I remember thinking my testimony was rather boring. I grew up in a Christian home. My parents stayed married. I left for college. No drama. How could I minister to others if I didn't have some chaos in my life to share how God had gotten me through it? I still feel extremely blessed today; yes, there have been challenges, but God has always remained been faithful.

While preparing your testimony, here are some factors to keep in mind:

- Don't read your testimony off of an index card. This is your story and it should be something that you can share without reading it word for word. If you need a note card with a few key points, that is okay.
- Pick a scripture that represents where you are at today and why you want to move forward with a small group. Go to biblegateway.com and look up different versions of the Bible if you want to compare some translations to find a scripture that perfectly conveys what you are trying to say.
- Don't use clichés. Be original.
- Be authentic. No one is looking for a perfect performance, but rather a sincere explanation of how you have reached this place in your life. You are there to explain why God has laid chronic illness ministry on your heart and the journey to this point.

Rick Warren recommends these 4 points to consider adding to your testimony:

1. What my life was like before I met Jesus?
2. How did I realize I needed Jesus?
3. How did I commit my life to Jesus?
4. What difference has Jesus made in my life?[2]

Preparing your vision statement to take to the church

Many churches ask people who are presenting an idea to the church for a new ministry to come up with a vision statement to bring to them. You may want to ask your church about what specifics they would like, but it's typically a one page document that explains your vision, your desire, and your plans. See an example in the appendix.

If your church says yes with enthusiasm

If your church is enthusiastic congratulations! It can be exciting to see the eyes of your church leadership light up as you are sharing your testimony. Many of them have either lived with chronic conditions or have seen a loved one who has lived with an illness. They may currently be a caregiver for a loved one and so personally understand that there is much more to this "illness thing" than one would know if they were on the outside looking in. They also are familiar with just how hard it can be to just get through each day when you live with constant pain. That you have chosen to allow God to use your pain in this way, to reach out to other people, can bring them great joy and appreciation.

If your church says yes, but reluctantly

Here is a scenario: Let's say you attend a traditional denominational church that would prefer that ministries first focus on getting people to come to church, but you would like your group to be an outreach tool. And though the church leadership typically would tell someone presenting a vision for a chronic illness small group that it should be for members only, you give them an emotional and compassionate presentation and they agree that you can move forward with the group. They even agree to let you announce it in the local paper under a support group listing.

Let's move forward six months from now. You have approached the church to share about the growth of your group and also ask for about fifty dollars in support to help you with some minor expenses and new leadership books. But the church leadership doesn't seem to be enthused and they have denied your request for funds. You are beginning to feel like you are on your own and without the emotional support from the church you'd hoped for.

You have posted a free announcement each week in the local paper and spread the word about the group at the local hospital and medical facilities. You meet on a monthly basis and have about fifteen people attending, about half who are currently not attending any church, and only about four who are members of your church. The group is going through their second Bible study and some people cannot afford it. You would also like a few leadership books to help you with the growing small group interactions and planning.

The church has only announced your group once in their bulletin and put the wrong date. When you asked the secretary about it, she said the church didn't even have an illness group, and you tried to explain, yes, they did . . . you were the leader. And she said, "Oh, I never realized that. I've had a few people ask if such a group existed, but I just said no." You are getting frustrated. The person answering the phones was not even aware of your ministry and you wonder what happened to the people who called to request information.

The church says you don't need more publicity; you already have the weekly post in the paper. And no, they don't have any financial support for the group. They are not interested in purchasing materials for people who aren't even attending the church. You try to explain that these people would *like* to attend, and some even log on and watch the web cast, but their illness makes it difficult to get up early on Sundays and some cannot even drive. You try to explain the transformation you have seen in people who have been attending now for six months. They have gone from being depressed and hopeless to disciples for the newer attendees and a real source of encouragement.

The leadership of the church says they refer people to the group all the time that come in for counseling and it's not their fault they aren't coming. They don't want to encourage people to come to your group necessarily because they are organizing a big healing service in a couple of months and would prefer people get excited about this, rather than accept living with their disease. They say you can continue to meet and have the room, but they aren't really interested in bringing in more people from the community who are not able to contribute to the church in either their presence or their financial gifts.

Although there are countless churches that are very much emotionally and practically supportive to group leaders, a situation like the one above is not unique. And for the leader it can be very exasperating. It's hard to be able to explain with words what you can see happening in the lives of people who are attending your group. Each week you see first-hand how God is literally changing their lives and you desperately wish for the church to be able to see the impact this group is having.

Take a moment to try to identify with those in your church leadership. People in any management positions, churches included, are often looking at the bottom line and although they can appreciate how God may be at work in the lives of people, they still must stay true to the mission that God has given their pastor. Too often they feel that committing money and publicity into a ministry they are not one hundred percent committed to is not fruitful. You may never encounter a situation like the one above, but if you do, be prepared to take it to the Lord in prayer instead of harboring resentment.

If your church says no

"My church said that they didn't feel like it was a good idea right now. I got the feeling they wanted me to be healed first, but they also said they really had not seen much of a need and they were being very particular about what new ministries they added right now. So now what? I was sure I'd felt God leading me to this." - Melinda

Many times, for a variety of different reasons, a church may actually say "no" or "not now." Don't take it personally (though it does hurt, I know.) Instead, consider that God may want you to go about following His calling in a way that you had not expected. You may want to start a community group, or you may just want to have a few people over to your home or out for coffee. Have a less formal environment and see where this leads. Pastor T. D. Jakes says, "As much as it pleases God to bless you, there will be moments when everything you try goes up in smoke. There will be moments when the one you counted on most walks away and leaves you groping through blinding tears and wailing questions of why. Plans and goals can be circumvented by the most disappointing of times, leaving you learning the art of patience and the acceptance of a denied request."

Deciding if you should move forward with your group

If your church either turns down your ministry idea, or accepts it but with a great deal of trepidation, you have a choice to make:

You can try to *force* the ministry upon the church. You may give a compelling testimony and they may approve it. The ministry may then succeed . . . or not. If your church is not supportive, it can be hard for the people within the church to believe the ministry itself is valued. But if you feel called to pursue your dream, at this church, God can work miracles despite the plans of man. Spend a great deal of time and preparation in prayer to do your best to hear God's voice if this is the path you are to take.

You can move to another church. Some people do actually determine that if the church they are involved in, dedicating their time to, worshipping at every week, does not have chronic illness ministry as one of their areas of concern and passion, then it's not the church for them. They may leave their church and start attending another church. Be aware, however, that all church leadership is justifiably apprehensive of brand new members who come into the church with a plan to immediately change or start a new ministry.

One thing to consider is the advice of Henry Blackaby, author of *Experiencing God*. He says:

> ". . . Jesus watched to see where the Father was working and joined Him. You can follow that same pattern by watching to see where God is at work around you. When He shows you, join Him in His work. Keep your attention on God;s call to an assignment rather than on your spiritual gifts, personal desires, skills, abilities, or resources. Once you understand God's call to an assignment, obey Him, and He will work through you to accomplish His divine, eternal purposes."[3]

Consider starting a community group

One of your options is to start a group in the community, separate from the church body. A number of illness groups and HopeKeepers groups have started as a community group. Although you won't have the benefit of having the church umbrella to assist you when problems arise, you may also avoid a few headaches and be able to have more control over your group and how it is managed. For example, you may find the church is very particular about whom they allow in to be a speaker at your church; some churches even require all speakers at the church building be of the same denomination. If you run up against some of these challenges, you may wish to consider announcing your group to friends, family, and local places, and meeting somewhere like the community library or a hospital meeting room.

At this point you may be eager to move forward and start planning your group meeting. . . or you may be closing the book and asking God, "What now? Do you want to me to lead a group? What should I pray for?"

I like this quote from Beth Moore: "If we are willing, we can also receive a new song from God that arises from hardship's victories, not necessarily in musical notes but in fresh truths engraved on the heart. These are precious gifts that eventually come to those who keep the faith and wait to see God redeem great difficulty. These songs can be heard by others but they cannot be learned secondhand."

God has given you a song. Spend time in prayer to find out how He desires you to share the music.

"I find that doing the will of God leaves me no time for disputing about his plans."
George MacDonald

"The grand essentials of happiness are: something to do, something to love, and something to hope for."
Allan K. Chalmers

"As a leader, it's your job to help your volunteers continue the healing process. Help them to see what God sees when He looks at them. Help them to use their hurt to help others whose scars are even fresher than their own."
Tony Morgan and Tim Stevens, Simply Strategic Volunteers: Empowering People For Ministry

"Preparation gives God room to work. When a leader is well-prepared, God has greater opportunity to work in the group. There are fewer distractions. Satan has fewer opportunities to get in and mess things up. The group flows more smoothly, allowing God to be the focus of the group."
Dave Earley, 8 Habits of Effective Small Group Leaders

CHAPTER 12

Preparing for your first meeting

The time has come to prepare for your first meeting. Take a deep breath and remember that it's not about perfection — it's about providing a place where people with illness can get together to fellowship and pray for one another's needs. Know that it's very likely something won't work out exactly as you had hoped, or that there will be moments of awkwardness. There will be times that you don't feel like you know what you are doing. Don't worry about it. God often has us in over our head so we must rely on Him.

Hebrews 11:7 tells us, "By faith Noah, when warned about things not yet seen, in holy fear built an ark to save his family." He didn't know what would come to pass, but he listened to God's commands and followed through, even when those around him ridiculed him.

Another good reminder is that God knows your timeline. In the midst of preparing for your first meeting you may suddenly have a bad flare or end up with emergency surgery and you feel frustrated that everything has been put on hold for weeks or even months. 1 Peter 3:20 reminds us, "God waited patiently in the days of Noah while the ark was being built."God gave the commands, watched Noah start drawing up plans and building the ark. . . and God waited patiently. If you are emotionally ready to go with your group, but something delays the process, know that God is still in control. He is waiting patiently for the day your group will come to pass. It may no longer be on *your* schedule, but God is never off *His* schedule.

Pray

It should come as no surprise that the first step towards preparing for your small group is to pray. In the rush and excitement of starting your group however, it can become easy to shoot little arrow prayers toward heaven with short pleas attached that read things like "Help!" or "Lord, please let someone be there," "I dedicate this small group to You, but You know how much work I put into it. Please let it go well." Be sure to put aside some time where you can actually sit down and have a conversation with the Lord that lasts longer than the red stop light at the intersection. It is a verse that we are all familiar with, but still need to be reminded: "But seek first His kingdom and His righteousness, and all these things will be given to you as well." (Psalm 94:11).

In a study completed by smallgroups.com they found that prayer actually has a measurable impact on a small group:

> "Research revealed absolutely zero correlation between time spent preparing the lesson and whether the group was growing in any way. In other words, when you statistically compare hundreds of leaders spending two hours preparing their lessons with hundreds of leaders spending five minutes preparing their lesson, there is no difference at all between those two groups in whether their groups are bringing more people to Christ, adding new members, or producing more leaders."[1]

But there are very high correlations when it comes to whether the group leaders are praying for their meetings.

Wayne Cordiero, author of *Leading on Empty: Refilling Your Tank and Renewing Your Passion* says, "Good intentions can fuel us in the beginning, but they won't last in the long haul. All of those good intentions and high self-expectations can eventually eat full-time shepherds alive when our expectations are inevitably disappointed."[2] Truly. . . turn it over to the Lord from the very beginning and you will avoid much heartache and stress.

Meet with your assistant

Who will be helping you? Who can assist you in setting up the meeting room, running errands, and making phone calls? Don't plan on taking on all of the responsibilities yourself. You will need the help and should give others the opportunity to be involved in this level with the group. If you don't yet have a co-leader you may want to at least have a couple of volunteers who rotate to help you at least with the administrative or physical tasks.

When you are chronically ill it can be draining to run to the other side of the church to make copies before the meeting starts. These kinds of responsibilities can be delegated, especially to a healthy person. You may even want to have your spouse or teenage child help you if they are willing. Before your meeting, sit down with someone, either your assistant, a pastor, or a dear friend, and just pour your heart out and dedicate this ministry to the Lord.

Meet with pastoral leadership

Go over any last minute questions you have. Make sure the group will be announced or in the bulletin as planned. Do any of your materials need to be reviewed, such as the letter from you in a welcome folder, your statement of faith, etc.?

Review the lesson you have chosen

If you have chosen to start off the first meeting with an actual lesson or study, be sure to spend some time reviewing it so you feel prepared. The first meeting may likely be more of a get-to-know-you time, however, you may want to have a Bible study that is ready to pass out to everyone and let them know what your expectations will be for the following week. I think it's important to also emphasize the fact that although you would like everyone to do the lesson and be prepared for the next meeting, that if they do not have a chance to complete it, they are still more than welcome to attend. Communicate to your members that you welcome their presence no matter what. The last thing you want are people who are unable to complete the study due to their medical condition skipping meetings out of shame or regret.

Make up a loose itinerary

Prepare an itinerary. It's great to have a plan, but don't be afraid to stray from it to allow the Lord to work in ways that are not on the agenda. Many people with illness cannot sit for extended periods of time, be gone from home for long, or go more than a couple hours without food. It's helpful to have a schedule they can look at so they know approximately what to expect. Remember, nothing is set in stone.

Feel free to have a very brief outline for the first group meeting and then ask participants what they are interested in. Some groups start with just listening to a special song on a stereo and they take turns bringing a CD of the song that gets them through the tough times. Others have a short worship time of one or two praise songs.

Here is the outline of a group that meets in California during the mornings.

10 - 10:45	Beverages and a light snack are provided
	Folks arrive and fellowship, noting prayer needs on Prayer Sheet provided
10:45 - 10:55	Stretch break
10:55 - 11:45	Bible Study, sharing (prayer needs recorded)
	A time of encouragement and loving each other
11:45-12	Prayer time
12 – 12:30	Folks are welcome to stay and fellowship

It's a good idea to have a definite time that people can feel free to leave and those who wish to stay and talk can feel welcome to do so. Remind people that everyone in the room has times of not feeling well, and that they can feel free to stand and stretch if they need to. They don't have to feel they must only stretch on schedule.

> "I find for us it works best if we keep to a routine. Our morning starts with 10 minutes of coffee time and chats to get to know specific needs to be prayed for that day. We then have our prayer time, which is vital to us; following this we have our study, which lasts around 30 minutes. I don't know about others but that is long enough for our restless bodies and minds. We usually have a time of games or quizzes. Since this is around a set time we do have a lady join us to chat and share who is not a Christian but we have been praying for." - Robynne

Order any materials or items you will need in plenty of time

If you are ordering any items for your meeting, such as Bible studies or books, be sure to do this a couple weeks in advance so they arrive in ample time. Rest Ministries has a variety of HopeKeepers logo merchandise to help your group feel like they are a part of something larger than just their individual group, if they would like. Mugs or travel mugs are a fun way to share morning coffee. Tote bags are available, that are great for all of your papers, Bible etc. And even balloons. These are fun to put helium in and pass out to those in your group while having a devotional time about how everyone in the group is there to "lift each other up." They are also fun for your resource table or parking lot area.

Put together welcome folders for new members

Many leaders put together an introductory packet for new members. This is a great way to have everything in one place and make sure that all members get the same information. When someone joins your group, especially if it is someone from the community who may not attend your church, this is a way the church can introduce themselves to the person in a non-threatening way. A letter from the pastor or a list of other ministries at the church may encourage them to get involved in other areas. Below are some suggested items to include in your welcome packet and you can add to it at any time with fresh resources.

- An introductory letter from you and from your pastor
- A list of participants and information they are willing to share such as phone numbers, addresses, email addresses, spouses, ages of kids, birthdays, good times to call, etc.
- An itinerary of the group session (such as scheduled meetings and fun activities)
- Information about your church such as a brochure or newsletter bulletin and a Rest Ministries brochure
- Informational sheet about a lending library of books, tapes, CDs, DVDs, etc.
- Devotionals from Rest Ministries web site or articles of interest

- A recommended reading list and sheet of inspiring quotes or scriptures
- Verse cards (available from Rest Ministries)
- Rest Ministries Viewpoint on Healing (see Appendix)
- A listing of your church ministries, who to call in case of an emergency, etc.
- Small items, such as stickers, a pen, note pad, note cards to send people encouragement, or a coupon to be redeemed for "a cup of coffee with you"
- Local resources with phone numbers for people with chronic illness that members may find helpful

Promotion

How do you plan to promote your group? If it's formed under the umbrella of another organization, what kind of approval do you need to advertise or use their name? Understand the specifics about what is acceptable or not. For example, are classified ads in the local paper or an announcement in the paper in the calendar section alright? Is it okay to post flyers around town? Make sure you know exactly what promotional pieces need advanced approval.

Start a box with everything you will take to the meeting

Put together a box of essentials. Take this box to every meeting. It should have nametags, pens, paper, handouts, new member folders, a sign in sheet, and napkins for snacks, tissues and whatever else you can think of. Be sure to include a bottle of hand sanitizer and a box of inexpensive pens. Encourage people to bring their own pens each time so you don't share germs.

Name Tags

It is a good idea to have some sort of sticker so people can have name tags at each get together, regardless of how long you have been meeting. Some people with chronic illnesses have cognitive challenges and have difficulty with memory. Others of us just forget. To increase the intimacy of the group, have people wear name tags so no one feels awkward when they forget a name of a member who has been there for months. It's also helpful when you have a speaker or special guest.

Remember to keep it perky

One of the fears I hear most often expressed is "What if everyone just comes and complains all the time?" Christian chronic illness small groups are supposed to be different than secular support groups—people are supposed to have hope! How will you add some fun to your group so it's not a depressing atmosphere or completely self-centered? Let everyone know that venting to a certain degree is understandable, but you don't want your group to just be a place people dump and then leave.

You'll most likely find that people are relieved to be able to express their feelings of bitterness, anger, and resentment, but that this often is diffused quite quickly when they finally are allowed to share these emotions in a safe place and have them validated. Working your way through a Bible study will help as well with this transition process. If a conversation begins to get out of control, as the facilitator you can say, "I think we're getting a little bit off course. Sara, can you read question number two to us? I think we can all relate with some of these bitter emotions, but let's see how God would like us to deal with them."

If you're looking for a book on this subject, *Lord, Change My Attitude Before It's Too Late* by James MacDonald, is an excellent source.

> "There were only four of us at the meeting, but it gave each a chance to share. A couple of the ladies in our group are new to our church. They left their former church in which they had been very involved due to a lot of problems. They discussed how they feel in a new church not being involved in anything and yet how afraid they are to get involved due to their physical problems at this time. I am working on some different ideas to present to them that they could do from home."
> —Linda

Ice breakers

Oftentimes it can be hard to get people to open up to one another when they first arrive at a group meeting. Or perhaps the people in your group have begun to form friendships, but when a new person arrives you notice that she feels somewhat uncomfortable.

Opening your meeting with some simple questions can be an excellent tool to get people to share a part of his or her self with others, without putting them on the spot. The questions are thought-provoking, yet not too personal. Encourage every person to answer a question and emphasize that their answer does not need to be illness-related, but it can be.

The first thing that comes to mind is. . .

You can have some real giggles as well as divulge some buried emotions just by passing out a bunch of random words. Make up a list of off the wall words to pass around. Have people share the first thing that pops into their head when they read it. Be both serious and silly in your choices.

Morning	Joy	M&Ms
Raindrops	Emotions	Tears
Prayer	Silly	Cabin
Mystery	Practical	Page-turner
Ketchup	Puppy	Backseat
Frustration	Candlelight	Highlighter
Anxiety	Low tide	Apple juice
Reality	Freeway	High maintenance
Separation	Electric	Staples
Wagon ride	Cupcake	Lemon Juice
Love Bug	Seeds	Life raft

Use material from the internet to start a conversation

Pass out a devotional or two from Rest Ministries' website (keep the author/copyright information on it too.) Have people read a paragraph out loud and discuss it. Have they ever felt this way? How did they cope with these feelings? Would they have done something differently had they read this first? If they had written this, what verse would they have chosen? What do they think of the way the writer responded to the circumstances or feelings that s/he encountered?

Encourage one another to not give up

Sometimes all it takes is a reminder from other people in the room that we have all had moments when we felt bummed out about living one more day with this illness. When needing to motivate one another, go around the room and share by having everyone finish a sentence you choose. This is one way to give all members a chance to talk, without forcing anyone to break too far out of their comfort zone. People can answer as simple or as revealing as they choose.

- One thing that I have let my illness prevent me from doing/being/saying, etc. is

185

_____.From now on I am going to

_____.

- If I could write the headline for tomorrow's newspaper it would be

_____.

- In the last 6 months, something I have learned is

_____.

- One thing I would love to do but I've not yet because I just wasn't sure if I could handle it is

_____.

Get creative!

Here is one of our favorite ideas that a HopeKeepers leader has sent to us:

> "I've started handing out 'Spiritual Vitamins.' At the end of every meeting each person takes out a 'vitamin' from the jar. It is filled with God's promises. Each reads their vitamin and we are amazed at how they speak to the things we have been talking about. I urge them to try to find someone to give that to during the week. They love that." -Nancy

Fun props

You can provide some props to make people smile. Go ahead and get silly and you'll be surprised to see how eager people are to join you. Visit your local dollar store or the web site of Oriental Trading Supply Company. They have many small silly items for just 25-50¢ each and you can buy a dozen at a time. Plastic frogs that can stand for "Fully Relying on God;" rubber noses — see who can wear it the longest while talking about being depressed, and not laugh! Order some fun Hawaiian items and have a "hang loose" theme for the study on surrendering everything over to God. Have a hat day or a "goofiest mug" day. Don't be afraid to get silly. You'll find that laughter will come from your group much more than you expect.

Let people know what to expect

Emphasize the fact that each person is there to find support and encouragement, while encouraging others. Although your group will discuss the various aspects of their illnesses, it's important that they refrain from comparing their physical limitations with one another. Medical support groups often fall into discussions of "How many surgeries have you had?" and "How much medication are you taking?" It becomes easy for people to feel as though they shouldn't be there, because (1) they aren't hurting enough; or (2) because they are in more pain than anyone else and no one really understands the severity of their pain.

Remember that this is just your first meeting and one small icebreaker could last you for most of the meeting, as people will enjoy getting to know each other and sharing their stories. Don't try to schedule in too many things, but rather allow the meeting to flow so that people understand the purpose of them being there, but that they also have the opportunity to express what they hope to gain from the time together.

*"If we're growing, we're always
going to be out of our comfort zone."*
John Maxwell

*"Greatness lies, not in being strong, but in the right
using of strength; and strength is not used rightly when
it serves only to carry a man above his fellows for his
own solitary glory. He is the greatest whose strength
carries up the most hearts by the attraction of his own."*
Henry Ward Beecher

*"Needless to say, you can love people without leading
them, but you cannot lead people without loving them."*
John Maxwell

*"God uses normal ordinary people in daily life. And
if God only used perfect people, nothing would get done.
Because none of us are perfect."*
Rick Warren

*"[Group members] must see how their contribution to
the team will help produce more and better fruit. They
must see how their gifts and passions will be used to help
the group grow. They must understand that I simply
cannot—and will not—lead alone any longer."*
Michael C. Mack

CHAPTER 13

Promoting your group and encouraging attendance

The announcements go out publicizing the beginning of the chronic pain ministry. And then the calls began.

- "I signed up for this because it sounded interesting, but I am in remission right now and I don't really feel like talking about my illness."
- "I'd really like to come, but I am so tired. I just can't make it tonight. Please forgive me."
- "I wish I could be there, but I have to work late tonight since I had a doctor's appointment this morning and I went home early yesterday. I'll try to make the next meeting, I promise!"

The problem with organizing a chronic illness or pain support groups are. . . *everyone is in pain* so there are challenges in getting everyone in one place. I'm not telling you this to discourage you, but rather so that you are not disapppointed when only a few people come. Some groups have a surprising twenty show up. . . others two.

As I was writing this book I asked group leaders to share with me what they would want to tell other leaders or potential leaders and repeatedly people shared, "Please tell other leaders not to be discouraged if attendance is low. Even if just one person comes you have made a difference in a life — and likely a new friend."

Attendance

So let's talk about attendance for a minute because this is perhaps one of the most basic, yet emotional parts of having a chronic illness small group. What happens when no one shows up or just one or two people come? Colossians 3:23 says, "Whatever you do, work at it with all your heart, as working for the Lord, not for me," and this is one of those areas we need to deliberately apply this scripture. Although we may be starting and leading this group for people, it should ultimately be because we feel we are glorifying God by following His calling to do so. He already knows how many people will be at your first meeting, your second meeting and so forth. He has written up the place cards and knows just who will attend, where they will sit, and what the conversations will be like.

But yes, it can be disheartening when attendance is low. And so far I have not determined any reason for the discrepancy, including the sizes of the churches. The only reason I can substantiate is that the Lord is responsible for bringing people to the group that He desires to have there. We have put so much effort and energy into preparing there is a "selfish" part of us that wants as many people to benefit as possible. Let's take a look at the experiences of some leaders:

> "At first I had problems finding interest at my church. I know that there are quite a few people who could benefit from a support group, but if they won't come there is nothing we can do. Sometimes I think it's a misconception about the format of the group. My solution was to go to the pastor in charge of the recovery/support group ministry at a local church. There are five of us [in the group] but we have really

connected with each other. Being small gives everyone a chance to share about their study that they are working on, as well as how their week went. We don't try to do a chapter a week. I let everyone work at their own pace. I believe God is ministering to each person this way. There is no pressure on anyone, especially when they don't feel well. I tell them just come so we can pray for them." -Venita

"There are five ladies in my group and we have a great time at our meetings. To those of you who are wondering how to advertise HopeKeepers, I've come to the conclusion that word-of-mouth is the best way. My church is a large one and I would've expected more to participate in HopeKeepers, but God sent these five ladies. None of them came because of my talks to different groups in the church, or handing out brochures or even from the letter I sent to every family in the church. They came because I or someone else knew they were ill and invited them personally. I guess it's hard to admit that you need a support group or maybe it's hard to let people in the church environment know that you have a chronic illness (you know - the old 'you would be well if you had enough faith stuff'). But this is God's ministry, not mine, and He'll get the people there who need to be there." —as posted on the HK Message Board

One person emailed me recently and poured out her heart about the attendance (or lack of) in her group: "Five people said they would definitely be there this week, but only one person ended up attending. I felt embarrassed, as this was her first visit and she was really looking forward to meeting other people. Am I doing something wrong? What can I do to get people to attend?"

First, I understand how frustrating this can be. A good scripture to cling to during times like this is 1 Peter 5:2. It says, "Be shepherds of God's flock that is under your care, serving as overseers—not because you must, but because you are willing, as God wants you to be; not greedy for money, but eager to serve."

In other words, follow God and be there for people when they show up. Avoid any feelings of irritation toward them when they are unable to come. People may not actually be blowing you off, but genuinely nervous about coming.

Here are some of the challenges that people face that prevent them from getting to the meetings. Consider what you can do to possibly increase the odds of them attending.

- **People are stretched to the limits in time constraints.** If a member is a mom, for example, she is probably coping with the guilt of not being able to always participate in her child's activities. If an evening comes along and she feels good, chances are she is going to stay home. She doesn't know when she will feel good again, and the chronic pain group will always be there.

- **People have different limitations.** Some people will be able to get in the car, drive fifteen minutes, and sit through a two-hour meeting. Others will not. Some will be able to do it easily. For some, it will take an enormous amount of energy to get there and participate. Everyone has his or her individual limitations.

- **People have their own body clocks.** Some people get up early in the morning and get as much done as they can because by noon their energy starts dissipating. Others will just be climbing out of bed at noon, and will finally be able to walk around by 5 p.m. You have the challenge of finding a meeting time that will best suit everyone who would like to attend.

- **People have different responsibilities.** Some people work full-time, some work part-time and some don't work at all. Again, finding a meeting time that works for as many as possible will be a challenge, but it is possible!
- **People who aren't currently in pain, won't want to come.** Who wants to think about pain any more than they must? You'll find that when people start to feel good, they may be less motivated to come. Accept this and keep in touch. At some point, they will want and need your support again.

Things that will encourage people to come

People who are hurting and going through physical (and emotional) pain will natually be drawn to a place that offers them unconditional love. James Friesen, and James Wilder, authors of *Living From the Heart Jesus Gave You: The Essentials of Christian Living* say, "People need to know who they are. They also need to be reminded who they are, frequently, by those who know them and really love them. And they need repair, so that they can live from the hearts Jesus gave them. That is what it takes to achieve wholeness in a fractured world. It takes belonging to a community."[1]

Below are my best tips to encourage people to come. Do what you feel comfortable with. Don't assume you must go down the list and force yourself to complete all the tasks. Rather, remember how one HopeKeepers leader said her attendees came because they were personally invited.

Make it easy for people to come

- Set up a meeting time that is consistent, such as "the first Tuesday of the month" so people always know when the meeting is and can plan on it each month.

- Describe in your announcement what the group atmosphere resembles. There will be many people observing so now is the time to let everyone know what you stand for.

Word-of-mouth

- Open up the group to people in the community. Oftentimes, a person may come to the church *because* of your group.
- Call local churches and hospitals and let them know that you have an illness small group.
- Invite spouses or loved ones to he meetings and encourage them to communicate with one another about their challenges, blessings, etc.
- Mention your small group to your physicians.
- Encourage your church's visitation ministry to tell others about the group.
- Make sure people in church leadership are aware of the small group, so that when they talk to someone who has a chronic illness, they can inform him of your small group.
- Go introduce yourself to the church secretary and bring her a small gift and a flyer with group meeting details so she remembers your ministry.
- Ask the church leaders if you can stand up during a service and announce the ministry and why you feel God has led you on this path.
- Include the topic of your next speaker in the church bulletin. People who may not currently be in pain may be encouraged to come and hear the presenter anyway.
- Talk a lot. Get a Rest Ministries t-shirt or other items that will make people stop you and ask questions, like a bumper sticker and carry verse cards (much better than a business card!) from comfortzonebooks.com .

- Whenever people ask about your illness turn the conversation around to what God is teaching you through it and how He's working in your group.
- Mention the existence and the need of the group to other church leaders. Many of their families will have illnesses and even if they feel it doesn't meet their needs, it may for someone that they know. Inform the women and men's ministry leaders so when people talk to them about their troubles, they can refer them to your group.
- Inform the local doctors, nurses, counselors, physical therapists, etc. that attend your church.

Places to post flyers or brochures
- At local Christian bookstores, Christian coffeehouses
- At community health locations such as fitness clubs, yoga studios, chiropractic offices, pools
- At your local hospital or doctor's office
- At your church's resource table

> Gayla shares, "Our group collects current magazines, then we print stickers with the information for our HopeKeepers group and place them over the address areas on the magazines. Then we place in area doctor's offices and emergency rooms. The current magazines are welcome and we get a bit of exposure too."

Get listed
- Have your group listed in the small group section of your church resource list.
- Request a special blurb in the church bulletin on Sunday about the group.
- Put an ad in your local papers, either secular or Christian. Skim through the whole paper. It may be able to be listed under health, religion, elderly, caregiving, etc.

- Post flyers with tear-off slips with your phone number or email address at local health clubs, rehabilitation clinics or senior centers where people may be looking at the bulletin boards.
- If you are a HopeKeepers group, contact Rest Ministries so you are placed on the web site map for people to find you.

Activities and events
- Are there people who you think may benefit but they don't think they need it, especially the elderly? Ask them if they would consider being on a 3-5 person panel and sharing with "younger folk" about how they've lived successfully with illness and what they would offer as advice for those tough times.
- Pay attention to specific dates and use these to boost your group at local events or to make an announcement at church. October is National Disability Awareness Month; November is National Caregiver's Month; May is National Fibromyalgia Awareness Month; September is National Pain Awareness Month and National Invisible Chronic Illness Awareness Week. The timing can make your group newsworthy!
- Invite speakers to come and lead a discussion on a variety of topics. For example, a Christian nurse or physical therapist may be able to offer a unique perspective on care.
- If your church has a ministry faire, be sure to have a table with brochures and newsletters to distribute.
- Plan a picnic.
- Have your group put together small comfort baskets for individuals who have expressed an interest, but who haven't been able to come yet.

- Whenever you hear about a local event in your area that you cannot attend or exhibit at, call to see if they have a general resource table and if you could have some flyers on it.

Contact the media

- Read the newspapers and whenever there is an article about some similar group, call them and tell them about your own. Connect with others. Also, keep track of the reporters and columnists that do these stories. Writers will often do similar topics of articles in the future.
- Send a letter to your local paper and include any photos. For an example press release see the Appendix.
- If you have a local Christian radio show send them a brochure and some information. Ask if you could be a guest on a radio program or if they have public service announcements, if they'd announce your group.

Online outreach

- Make a video with your group's photos or short video clips, add music, and put it on a DVD for just $5 at Animoto.com. Nonprofits can get a free account.
- Use social networking to spread the word. Create "an event" on Facebook and tell all your friends. Twitter about your meetings, before and after, to increase interest. Post photos of your group's meeting or activities.
- Tape your group members can giving their best advice for living with illness or their testimony and then allow you to post on YouTube to gain exposure.
- Propose an article for your church's web site about your experience living with chronic illness and at the end encourage others to come to the group.

Brainstorm

- Make a list up of all of the reasons that people don't come and then write down a way that you can address this. What have people said when they have told you, "I'd like to come to a meeting but _____ "
- If people have signed up for the group, but they aren't coming, have the group members sign and send a card.
- Take time to find quality, sincere volunteers who want to be a part of a ministry that will make a difference.
- What ways can your group members encourage others to attend? Brainstorm together how you can have more members if this is your desire.
- Although your focus is on developing the small group ministry, keep an active list of needs people have and how the church could further expand their illness ministry and outreach when the time is right.

"I was in the hospital recently and the hospital channel was on - the notice about our HopeKeepers group and meetings came up. That's thanks to one of the administrative assistants at church who sees that the info gets into every radio, print and TV calendar in the area. At a time when I was really sick for a few days, it brightened my day to know that our announcement was running at the hospital where many people will see it." - Rev. Karen M Clarke, MA HopeKeepers Leader, First-Plymouth Congregational Church

Promotional pieces

What kinds of promotional pieces do you need to help promote the group and who can design them? Things like posters, flyers, business cards, and stickers, can all be very useful in spreading the word about your group. Ask if anyone does design or digital scrapbooking for help and ideas. Most items can be printed on your home printer. If your group is a HopeKeepers group, Rest Ministries has pre-printed business card and posters where you can add you group's information. See chronicillnessbooks.com.

Create an awareness event

> "In 2001, our group sponsored a 'HopeKeepers® Day' where our goal was to reach out to other churches and let them know of the value of HopeKeepers groups. One of the leaders from another group came, along with the leaders of a local ministry that have been of great support to me and this ministry. Although the turnout was meager one woman began a group as a result and now has three groups going in New Hampshire! I still have a deep desire to get the word out on how important these support groups can be." - Cindy

Prepare a press release and send it out

Many group leaders have had their local newspaper do a profile piece on them. They aren't seeking personal glory, but rather a way to get the word out about the group. I encourage you to send out a press release to local newspapers, including both Christian and secular, as well as local Christian radio stations.

Many radio stations have guests for their talk radio programs and are interested in letting their audience know about local ministries.

Check with your church about who may be able to guide you in getting the word out. The church may have some personal contacts at newspapers, television stations and radio stations. The press release in the Appendix can easily be adapted for your personal use, just add your own quotes. SBwire.com offers free press releases to nonprofits, so you may want to ask your church to sign up for an account.

Tips for working with media

- Send out a letter/press release to your local talk radio stations and newspapers. Christian media may be especially interested in hearing your story about living joyfully despite having a chronic illness. Look in the Yellow Pages for phone numbers and email addresses.

- Media representatives are busy people; therefore keep your press release to one page. Remember who, what, when, where, why and how. Who is your target audience?

- Make your heading catchy and unique, but descriptive.

- When do you want people to know about your event? If you want to get as many people involved as possible, a press release can be sent out at any time.

- Double check your spelling, your sources, back up any statistics you use by providing the source. Be accurate and the media will appreciate you!

- Ask around to see if friends or family have media contacts. Be sure to follow up any inquiries and provide additional material, statistics or quotes where needed.

- Remember to thank media representatives and programs, which have been helpful and establish connections for next year.

Michael C. Mack offers this advice regarding small group growth:

> "In many small groups led by solo leaders, the leader is the only one who 'recruits' or invites people to the group. This is inefficient and often ineffective. The core group takes ownership right away by praying and then inviting people in their spheres of relationship into the group. This act is also vital for

how group members will be shepherded and discipled in the future."[2]

Finding a balance between working toward growing your group and yet focusing on the people and not the numbers is a challenge. Through prayer for your group members and a close connection with the Lord, you will find that He will build it and He will send those people to it that He desires to have there.

"When a leader admits to his or her weaknesses, they are inviting others to participate in leadership to fill the gap of what the leader cannot do. No one can do everything, and this kind of vulnerability allows for everyone on a team to contribute in meaningful ways."
Nancy Ortberg

"Care for the flock that God has entrusted to you. Watch over it willingly, not grudgingly— not for what you will get out of it, but because you are eager to serve God. Don't lord it over the people assigned to your care, but lead them by your good example."
Michael C. Mack

"Make it a rule, and pray to God to help you to keep it: Never, if possible, to lie down at night without being able to say: 'I have made one human being at least a little wiser, or a little happier, or at least a little better this day.'"
Charles Kingsley

CHAPTER 14

Group maintenance: When things get difficult

So your group is meeting and people are coming (or maybe not. . .) and you are wondering how to meet some of the challenges you are now facing. There are a wide variety of books available that can help you in these steps, some of which are listed in the Resources chapter of this book. Below is a quick reference to evaluate your meetings, but I also encourage you to take a more extensive evaluation questionnaire at Christian author Douglas Britton's web site.[11]

How to evaluate your meetings

- Do you start and finish on time?
- Do you provide welcome materials for new members?
- Do you encourage your members to bring their Bibles?
- Do you give them something to take with them that will be encouraging for the following week, such as a devotional, poem, or scripture to look up?
- Do you have enough time to pray?
- Do you and your members keep everything that is shared in the group confidential?
- Do you have a time of worship or sharing praises?

---

[11] http://tinyurl.com/yzzudmt

- Do you keep a list of questions to ask your church leadership or other HopeKeepers leaders?
- Do you make sure that the members receive the contact information of other group members who are willing to share it?
- Do you plan activities to outreach to others who are hurting and not members of the group?
- Do you share your praises and problems in the HopeKeepers forum in the Sunroom or other area where you get leader support?

4 challenges to expect

You have put your heart and soul into planning and preparation for your group, so having it run less than perfect can be frustrating. Recognize that all the plans in the world cannot prevent a few of those unforeseen situations. Being aware of some of the hurdles you may encounter can help you be prepared in advance.

There are many books out there that will tell you how to lead an effective support group. You will find that parts of most of them will apply and be very helpful; however, leading a group for those with chronic illness has its unique challenges. Don't be discouraged, but rather, prepared. Here are a few of the challenges I'd like to personally address to defuse their power to dishearten you while you are in the thick of leading a group.

1. Only a couple of people come

How it feels: Disappointing

After all the work you put into it, not to mention the passion you feel about doing this, it can seem like a waste to just have one or two people show up. Understand that this can be typical, especially at first, when everyone feels a bit intimidated. Try not to take it personally

What to do: A good motto to remember is, "Hope for the best and prepare for the few."

It can be such a letdown when you feel God leading you to start a group and then only one person shows up. But from personal experience I can say that God knows what He is doing and may have planned it that way!

Keep an outline of your lesson and include what kinds of topics people shared. This way you can easily "repeat" the meeting with little preparation as a follow up. You may want to call people and, without pressuring them, ask if there is anything that you can do to make it easier for them to attend. Do they need a ride? What is typically a good time of day for a meeting?

2. Your lesson plan is completely ignored

How it feels: As though your ideas aren't interesting or inspiring enough to keep their attention.

It can also feel like the time you spent in preparation isn't appreciated.

What to do: Allocate more than usual flexibility in your timeline at first, and then add more structure as the group meets and you begin to see how it flows.

It's most likely that people are so excited to meet one another who understand what they experience living with daily chronic pain, that they just want to talk. You've provided a forum where the floodgates of pent up emotions are sure to spill over as soon as they realize they are allowed to be honest and vulnerable. It's impossible and impolite to hold up the Bible study book and insist you get back on schedule when a member is sobbing about her daughter who has told her mom her illness is "all in your head." This type of situation can occur at any meeting, but it may be more frequent during the first month.

Talk to your group about your desire to allow people to share, but also that you want everyone to leave feeling refreshed. So regardless of what happens during the meeting, you will plan to end with an uplifting article, scripture, poem, or devotional, and of course, prayer.

3. **Everyone complains about relationships, the medical professionals, their illness—everything.**

How it feels: Sometimes, like you are surviving a small mutiny
You will find many emotions that have not been expressed until now. People have deep wounds about things people have said to them or how they've treated them; unjust consequences due to their illness; perhaps even medical errors. It may feel like they want you to fix the chaos or else they will talk incessantly about it until you do.

What to do: Write up some guidelines, before your first meeting
If possible include "venting guidelines." Get creative in how to meet people's needs without straying from your mission statement.

One practical tool is to set a timer and allow everyone to have 60 seconds to share their most frustrating experience of the week. Brainstorm about a contest your group could have that would bring some humor to the venting. For example, the person who handled their irksome situation the best or most creatively could win the "Aggravated the Alligator (a rubber alligator) Award" to take home for the week.

Group members should have a sense of freedom in sharing their concerns and annoyances, but be sure to include others in the conversation. If Jane can't seem to let go of a situation, add, "Jane, I know some of us can identify with what you are sharing. Can someone else tell us how she or he has dealt with the emotions that accompany a situation that was similar?" If you are doing a study you can say, "Since we want to have plenty of time at the end to share something uplifting, let's move on to question five. Jane, would it be okay if people could offer their encouragement after the meeting or maybe later this week with a phone call or email?"

4. One person continually dominates the conversation—and it's not pretty

How it feels: Exasperating!

You imagined the group's conversations being balanced, full of grace, and encouraging so it can be annoying to have someone take the group down a path that lacks the encouragement you have planned to provide. She basically tries to control the meetings and completely interrupts people who are trying to talk. You justifiably are concerned about her impact on the group and how many people she could scare away.

What to do: Set boundaries at the beginning

It's important that people in the group are allowed to share their frustrations, but they also need to respect the others in the group. They must watch their language, the amount of time they dominate a conversation, and how they talk about other people's treatments or decisions.

One of the best ways to approach setting boundaries is to include guidelines about how the group will function that are given to all new members. If the person who dominates the conversations doesn't understand your simple comments of "Let's see how other people feel" then talk to her one-on-one. Politely go over the guidelines. Having the guidelines to refer to will make it feel less of a personal attack than if you are simply correcting her behavior.

You may want to put her in charge of a part of the meeting where she can have a specific responsibility such as leading the ice breaker time. Many times you can take the energy and passion of someone and turn it into a strength for the group and the individual.

Learning to Lead

Don't be too hard on yourself. Dave Earley shares in his book *The 8 Habits of Effective Small Group Leaders*, "When Joel Comiskey studied 700 small leaders in eight distinct cultures, he "discovered that the potential to be a growing, successful, small group does not reside with the gifted, the educated, or those with Type A personalities. The answer, rather, is hard work.'"[1]

You will learn as you go. Facilitating a support group is often assumed to be a simple undertaking. It's a myth that all one does is announce a meeting, lots of people attend, everyone shares and supports one another, and no personality conflicts arrive. That is impossible.

An effective support group leader is a special person who can effectively communicate with people, offer mentorship, grace, humility and authenticity. A facilitator must be able to gently guide people in the path she wishes them to go, so that the group makes a positive emotional impact. A leader must be compassionate, but also able to set boundaries or diffuse anger. As circumstances arise, ask other leaders for ideas and support. And most of all, remember that no leader ever feels one hundred percent capable. Having a willingness to learn and listen are some of the top leadership qualities in which to invest.

14 ways to perk up your program

If your group is suffering from the doldrums you may need some refreshment. Group routines can be helpful, but eventually they become just that. . routine! When your group members skip a meeting do they wonder what they missed? Or do they know exactly what they missed and they aren't concerned about it? Add some perk and soon people will be showing up again to participate.

1. **Change the environment or atmosphere**. If you normally meet at the church, meet in a home and open the meeting up to be less formal. Ask the group if this would work for them and be sure to meet in a home where there is plenty of comfortable seating and nearby parking. When the sun starts coming out, consider meeting one afternoon at a local park. If meeting elsewhere isn't an option, change the atmosphere. Bring in a boom box and have some energizing music playing as people arrive. If you meet at tables, have a little flower centerpiece or something. Coming up with these ideas may be a special ministry opportunity for someone to serve in the group.

2. **Switch the materials**. If you normally work from a Bible study, try a book. Bring in a speaker. Have a panel of people that can share what they know. Is there a doctor or pharmacist that would sit on panel? What about a pastor from your community who has an illness or who has a wife with an illness? Don't be afraid to try new materials or to do presentations in a new way.

3. **Skip a meeting and do something fun.** Go to a restaurant. Get tickets to a local event and call ahead for disabled access seating. It doesn't have to be a serious outing. Be adventurous and take your group to do something silly that no one has done for a while like

pizza at Chuck E. Cheese or sodas at a local bowling alley. Get people to laugh. Ask everyone to share his or her most embarrassing moment from high school or as a parent.

4. **Mix up the meeting.** Move worship to the end. Or sing the whole night long. Have one meeting be on the topic of prayer. Put aside the meeting agenda and just let people share. What is one thing they learned this year that they want to share with everyone? When was the last time they surprised someone and what was his or her response to the surprise? Have each person bring a keepsake or memento that is special to them to share about.

5. **Meet your neighbors.** Invite another small group to join your HopeKeepers group one evening for snacks and socializing. Oftentimes people think the chronic illness group must be depressing. Show them otherwise! Even better, invite a local secular support group that meets nearby to join your group one evening to share encouragement.

6. **Choose an activity.** Just because your group is made up of people with illness doesn't mean that you can't serve others. It can energize a group to know that they can make a difference in the lives of someone as a group, when they can't as an individual due to a lack of energy, time or resources. Discuss what kind of mission your group would like to have. Is there a homebound person your group could adopt? There are women in prison that have chronic illnesses that could be reached through Prison Fellowship Ministries. What about a parent who has a child with chronic illness? Notes of encouragement from your group or a care basket of goodies can make all of the difference in the life of someone hurting and feeling alone.

7. **Make faces!** Before your meeting, cut out some smiley faces and sad faces and glue them on each side of a stick or a plastic knife. When everyone goes around the room to share about their experiences or emotions of the week, ask people to make sure they are able to hold up both "faces". For example, Beth may say, "I'm not looking forward to my joint replacement surgery and all the rehab following" while holding up the sad side of the stick. And then she flips it to think of something positive to say such as, "I feel blessed though. The insurance is covering a lot of the expenses and my friends have volunteered to help take care of my children."

8. **Rethink your definition of what counts as indoor games for small groups.** For example, ask everyone to bring an item to contribute to a JOY box and then pass it around during the meeting and let people choose everything to take home. The range of objects can be anything: a silicone bracelet, a favorite poem, a funny DVD, an encouraging note or even a joke book. Have everyone return the item during the next meeting and occasionally have people bring fresh items.

9. **Be goofy together with ice breakers for small groups.** Make up a fun, corny theme song to start each meeting, or pick a tune everyone knows and make up new lyrics. Check out the web sites of Christian comedians for ideas.

10. **Find some goofy props to bring to your meeting.** Don't make anyone feel they must use or wear them. (Forcing someone to wear bug antennas may scare them away for good.) But make sure they are available to encourage light-hearted moments before discussing the depressing reasons you are there.

11. **Ask everyone to bring an item to include in a gift basket to encourage someone else.** It may be someone who

cannot attend the group someone having surgery, or a friend of someone recently diagnosed. Put your ideas together about things people would like. Don't forget personal notes or even sticky notes on a small gift can mean the most.

12. **Have items on hand that will encourage people to thrive despite their illness.** For example, National Invisible Chronic Illness Awareness week has fun things like bumper stickers, pins, mugs and stickers that have themes like "My illness is invisible but my hope shines through."

13. **Think positive.** When you schedule guest speakers, remind them that you want to provide the most positive outlook as possible, while still being practical. Invite them to pass out props or encouraging articles. Listen to your speakers before scheduling them. Some illness speakers are quite depressing.

14. **Sit down with your group and discuss what kinds of things you could do to create change.** Illness often robs people of feeling useful. Even though your group may not be able to physically walk for a charity event, you could work at a registration table or distribute water. Teens with chronic illness are often a great inspiration in getting a support groups involved in a higher calling. Remind people they can be part of something positive.

Support groups can provide some of the most influential relationships that can help one live successfully with chronic illness. The environment of the group, however, can make or break its usefulness. With these few simple tips, your group can be a refuge and a place of true relaxation, creating an special group for people to create friendships that could just last as long as the illness, perhaps indefinitely.

Oftentimes when a person has an illness and is involved in a small group, surrounded by healthy individuals, the ill person may still feel like he is burdening the others with constant prayer requests about his physical condition. The group of people may kindly listen, but they still can't grasp what the ill person is going through, the challenges he or she faces, and the many choices that must be made. In a **HopeKeepers** small group, one can openly express these feelings and the group can gather around each individual and say, "We understand," and truly mean it.

Recognizing your personal needs

There may come a time when you feel that your passion is fading. Maybe your illness has moved into a new season and needs to take top priority while you are in survival mode. Perhaps your family needs you right now in some role as a parent, spouse, or caregiver. Don't hesitate to take a sabbatical if you need to.

If you're group wants to continue meeting a co-leader may be able to step up or perhaps even a member could lead it. They could also have more speakers come and do more social outings for a season.

By being a leader you are producing fruit, so what do you do when you start to feel blue or overwhelmed during your fruit-producing moments? It's a sign to step back and re-evaluate if you need a sabbatical or if it's time to pass the group leadership to someone else.

Rick Warren shares in his book *The Purpose-Driven Life: What on Earth am I Here For?* how busy-work can move our purpose aside and tire us out: "Knowing your purpose motivates your life. Purpose always produces passion. Nothing energizes like a clear purpose. On the other hand, passion dissipates when you lack purpose. Just getting out of bed becomes a major chore. It is usually meaningless work, not overworked that wears us down, saps our strength, and robs our joy."[2]

A life-changing book if you are feeling burnt out is *Leading on Empty: Refilling Your Tank and Renewing Your Passion* by Wayne Cordeiro.

"Through thick and thin, keep your hearts at attention, in adoration before Christ, your Master. Be ready to speak up and tell anyone who asks why you're living the way you are, and always with the utmost courtesy" (1 Peter 3:15, *The Message*).

Remember not to put too much pressure on yourself! God is in charge and "able to do immeasurably more than all we ask or imagine, according to His power that is at work within us" (Ephesians 3:20).

"When you're burned out, problems seem insurmountable, everything looks bleak, and it's difficult to muster up the energy to care— let alone do something about your situation."
Michael C. Mack

"Disciples cannot be mass produced. We cannot drop people into a 'program' and see disciples emerge at the end of a production line. It takes time to make disciples. It takes individual, personal attention."
Leroy Eims

"The heart of the discerning acquires knowledge; the ears of the wise seek it out" (NIV)
"Wise men and women are always learning, Always listening for fresh insights" (The Message).
Proverbs 18:15

"Come and let us return to the Lord, for He has torn us so that He may heal us; He has stricken so that He may bind us up."
Hosea 6:1

CHAPTER 15

Frequently asked questions

Here are some of the questions that many small group leaders have.

Sometimes people start talking about how the church doesn't understand chronic illness and although I agree with some of what they are saying, I feel uncomfortable speaking of our church this way. I want to let them express their feelings though. What do I do?

It's no secret that there is often a lack of communication between church members and people who live daily with pain and it's only natural that this subject will come up in your group. However, I agree: the group setting is not a place to "bad-mouth" anyone, nor is it a place to come and just gossip about our frustrations.

One of the best ways to keep your group on track is by using the Bible studies as an outline for the meeting. It's often easier to say, "Let's move on to number four" rather than say, "We shouldn't talk about this!"

In the Bible study *When Chronic Illness Enters Your Life,* chapter 5 addresses how sometimes people don't understand chronic illness. It allows your group to discuss some of the things that people say that are hurtful and share their experiences. Knowing we are not isolated in our experiences is helpful. The chapter, however, also addresses why friends are special to us. It asks us to think of someone who has been an influential friend in our life.

The end of the chapter concentrates on how we can take action: How can we become a better friend? What steps can we take to improve our friendships, despite the illness? Rather than getting caught up in the idea that everyone should please us, we need to concentrate on what we can do to improve our relationships.

Ephesians 4:29 says, "Do not let any unwholesome talk come out of your mouths, but only what is helpful for building others up according to their needs, that it may benefit those who listen." Remember that there are people there who may not have socialized with Christians before or maybe not for many years. You cannot necessarily control every word that comes out of the mouths of your members, but you can gently remind them that speaking with the intent of gossip will not be something you will permit.

You want everyone to leave feeling renewed and replenished. No amount of "venting" will ever make us feel this way—it must always come back to how God can make a difference in the worst of circumstances for us to leave feeling hopeful and not hopeless.

Excellent resources that addresses complaining that you may find helpful are *Lord, Help Me Change My Attitude Before it's Too Late* by James MacDonald and my book *Why Can't I Make People Understand? Discovering the Validation Those With Chronic Illness Seek and Why.*

Sometimes it seems like people are getting depressed, and I don't know what to do to make them cheer up without sounding fake. Any ideas?

Yes! One of the best ideas that I've heard of was a Joy Box. Some people have started out with a joy file, and then it expands to a joy box. Late author and Christian humorist, Barbara Johnson had an entire room dedicated to things that made her laugh. But a small box is a great place to start. Who says joyful things are always flat?

Tell each person to bring a shoebox-sized box to the next meeting and then you bring the first item of joy. It can be the same item for everyone or different things for each person—a token item that fits his or her personality. Tell them that by the next meeting they should have their box decorated so that when they look at it it makes them smile and then encourage them to bring an item for someone else's box. It can be a goofy card, or a newspaper clipping with a funny title. Maybe it's a cartoon or something from childhood like a pet rock. It can even just be a notecard of encouragement or a chocolate bar (...if the person can eat chocolate!) Don't scare people away by making it too complicated! Keep it simple.

Tell your group they are to fill up their own joy box too with any little thing that makes them smile. Each week have everyone bring his or her Joy Box and share something out of it at some point during the meeting.

When I asked friends to share some things that they would include they suggested:

- movie stubs from a child's film they had to see (even though they were the only adult there without a child)
- a videotape of their favorite cartoons that still makes them laugh
- thank you cards from people for the gifts that they have sent
- colored-drawings from nieces and nephews
- favorite photos—especially those silly ones
- Silly Putty®, Slime® and a Rubix Cube®

- a list of all the things she wants to do before she dies (also known as a "bucket list")
- funny-looking little trinkets
- a hospital bill stamped "paid in full"
- a CD of favorite songs that cheer one up

I look forward to hearing what appears in the Joy Boxes from your group. You'll find that as one shares his or her own ideas about what brings them joy, others will get excited and think of more ideas too. They'll also get to know one another even better. Do you even know what really brings your very best friend true joy?

I hope that your boxes will "overflow with hope" (Romans 15:13) as well as joy!

I find that it's hard to get people to come to the small groups when they don't feel well, and yet when they do feel well, they don't want to talk about the pain! But they all say that they want to be involved. . . What do I do?

Each individual has various factors that influence whether they attend or not. While it's important to stress that the group will form tighter bonds and intimacy if everyone is there, it's also necessary to realize that the last thing you want to do is become "one more thing" that the person has to attend or one more thing to feel guilty about.

In Bill Donahue's book, *Leading Life-Changing Small Groups,* he shares how the leader must seek to find a balance of shepherding with both care and discipleship.

> "Practice intentional shepherding. Groups that help one another grow while also providing care for people in need will rarely have attendance problems. When we care for one another we declare that the church is a family. When we disable one another for ministry and

growth, we are equipping soldiers for the battle. Every leader must face the tension of how much effort to place on caring for people and how much time developing them. Intentional shepherding occurs when leaders encourage group members to consistently practice both. The Scripture says, 'Encourage one another and build each other up'" (1 Thessalonians 5:11).[1]

The first thing I would ask is how often are you meeting? Find a compromise about how often you meet; for some groups once a month is plenty and people tend to make sure that they get there. For others, that's not enough and the group wants to meet every other week. Find a balance that works for your group. Discuss what kind of commitment they can make and what kind of support they are searching for and expecting.

Remember. . . "each one can reach one." God has something planned for the one individual that shows up and a wonderful conversation can come from this time spent together. If just one or two people attend, you may ask them if they would like to work through the Bible study or if they would prefer to just talk a while and end in prayer. Let the Holy Spirit lead you where you need to go and don't get caught up in the quantity, but rather the quality.

Lastly, encourage attendees to invite others and bring their spouses. Take a moment to send out reminder postcards about 10 days before the meeting and emphasize what the topic of conversation will be.

For example:

Do you feel no one understands? Do you get hurt by the things people say? Join us as we go through chapter five of the Bible Study "When Friends Just Don't Understand."

If someone attends once, but then not again for awhile, keep sending him postcards. I had a woman attend who I hadn't seen for seven months and she said, "I never would have come if you hadn't kept sending me the postcards. Thank you!"

You may ask for people to call if they are not going to be able to attend, but remember that they are people who live with chronic pain, and they just may not get to the phone.

Low attendance does not necessarily mean a lack of interest, so don't take it personally. Some people have a deep desire for the community of the group and will be there no matter what. Others decide they would rather not discuss their illness and prefer to just get our newsletter or attend occasionally. As we journey down this path of chronic illness our needs will change as well. Keep on keeping on—when people need you they will be so glad that your group is still there waiting for them!

There are some people in my group who seem to talk a lot and others who really don't say much at all. How do I encourage everyone to participate without hurting anyone's feelings or putting anyone on the spot?

Most people who will come to your group will likely not have been in a support group setting for awhile, so you will have people who have been literally been waiting years to talk about the pain, and those aren't really comfortable talking about it at all yet.

As the leader you are in the position where you need to keep the group balanced. I often will tell "a talker," "That's really interesting . . ." and then ask, "Does anyone else have something that she would like to share?" If I know a particular person is comfortable talking, I may specifically ask her, "Shelly, do you have anything that you would like to add?"

In *How to Lead Small Groups*, Neil McBride, gives 6 tips on how to help people be comfortable.

1. *Set an example.* You must be willing to share (even if it means sharing that you are in pain!)
2. *Be patient.* It may take weeks before some people tell you what their illness is.
3. *Stress honesty.* Get down to the grit of it all so people feel that everyone is genuine.
4. *Practice acceptance.* Don't act shocked when people share surprising information.
5. *Accept differences.* Some people will be very verbal and others will not.
6. *Avoid pushing.* Don't force anyone to share. Some people learn best by listening.[2]

I also recommend reading some books on personality styles by best-selling Christian authors Florence and Marita Littauer. They offer priceless insight . By understanding the personalities of those in your group, you will be better able to predict what will draw people out. If you're trying to figure out why one particular woman always seems depressed and her spouse is excessively cheerful, the personality books will be helpful in gaining awareness about how to best approach them with both friendship and Bible study instruction.

We have a limited amount of time for our meetings since so many people don't feel well. We always close in prayer. However, by the time we get done going around the circle and hearing everyone's prayer requests, there is hardly any time left to pray. Some people's requests also start turning into lifetime histories. I don't know how to refocus it back on God when they are pouring their heart out.

I can imagine that there must be times when prayer time is completed and God says to Himself, "Gee, how come they talk to each other for two hours and me for two minutes?" Here are some ideas to make sure that you spend time with God.

First, explain when prayer time will be and how much time you will designate toward prayer. Emphasize your desire that the group really spends time with God and doesn't fall into the trap of just talking about God.

Spend 20-30 minutes in prayer and break it up in 5-10 minute "sessions." Spend five minutes worshipping and praising God, five minutes praying for someone beside you, and five minutes praying for your church or another ministry.

I once had a friend who kept multicolored index cards on a big ring with all of the things that she prayed for each day. Different colored cards even represented different areas of prayer (green for family, pink for health, etc.) Give everyone a stack of index cards and tell them to bring their area of needed prayer written down on a card the next week and exchange it with someone. Pray for spouses, parents, children, co-workers, caregivers, nurses, medical staff, and more.

You can split up into groups of 3-4 people. Even if you all share as a group, you can close in prayer in smaller groups and be more personal in what people talk to God about.

Don't forget to share praises of prayer that were answered. This may be a great way to start the meeting, or perhaps you can have someone share their praise as you are ready to start prayer time.

Too often prayer time ends up looking more like a list of all the things wrong in our lives and how we want them fixed by God's wave of His hand.

As hard as it may seem, make sure to make prayer time top priority. Imagine if you went to a birthday party and you ate the cake and ice cream, played all the games, and took home the favors, but you never said hello to the person you were there honoring.

During the group meeting everyone raves about how much they are enjoying the group, but then one by one they call me or email me to tell me that they think one person is talking too much or they think we should only have it be church members, or whatever. No matter what I do it seems they aren't really happy and that they want to do things differently. I'm tired of trying to please everyone.

Warren Wiersbe, Christian author of *The Bumps are What You Climb On*, once said, "The way we respond to criticism pretty much depends on the way we respond to praise. If praise humbles us, then criticism will build us up. But if praise inflates us, then criticism will crush us; and both responses lead to our defeat."

Expect criticism. There will always be a few that say you are giving up or giving in; that you are turning your back on God, abandoning them mid-stream. Don't feel you have to offer in depth explanations or excuses. It's between you and the Lord. The author of *Jesus on Leadership* shares,

> "Jesus' mission was not to fulfill wishes of those who followed him. His mission was to carry out the will of the Father. Too many leaders fail when they leave the mission to please their followers. This is why Jesus continually corrected His disciples when they (Peter, in particular) try to keep Him from suffering and dying to bring salvation to his people. His mission was to lay down His life as a sacrifice to bring a right relationship between God and all creation. His followers had to

understand His mission before they could understand their own. [3]

Rather than focusing on the negative aspect, let's flip it around and do what Jesus would do. Pray for them.

One of the most vital things you can do is to pray for the members of your group daily. Dave Earley, author of *The 8 Habits of Effective Small Group Leaders,* says this about prayer:

> "Prayer is a fascinating tool for the person with a heart to minister to others. It is one of the simplest things we can do. All we need to do is sit down and lift someone up to the attention of God. Yet most of us will admit that it is one of the hardest things to do for others. We get busy. We get distracted. We get discouraged, and we just don't pray enough. Highly effective small group leaders view prayer as a non-negotiable aid in their ministry to others. They use it often and well. They build it into their daily schedules and make it a high priority. They don't just pray a little; they pray a lot." [4]

"I had to be healed of my desire to be healed."
Joni Eareckson Tada

"We must accept finite disappointment,
but never lose infinite hope."
Martin Luther King, Jr.

"But faith is measured not by our ability to
manipulate God to get what we want but by our
willingness to submit to what he wants. It takes
great faith to say to God, 'Even if you don't heal
me or the one I love. . . I will still love you and
obey you and believe that you are good. And I
believe that You, as my loving Father, will use
everything in my life—even the hard and hurtful
things—for my ultimate good, because You love me.'"
Nancie Guthrie, Hearing Jesus Speak

"If we believe all our suffering is the devil's doing,
that our primary, possibly our only, motive is to get
rid of it. But if we see God in it, that makes a
difference. Our primary motive is not to get rid of
suffering but to find what God is trying to say to us."
Ron Dunn, Will God Heal Me?

"Silence is healing for all ailments."
Hebrew Proverb

CHAPTER 16

Answering tough questions: Where is all the healing?

God can heal. God is capable of taking a person out of the depths of life-threatening illness to wellness in a mere moment. So why doesn't He? Why doesn't He heal more people? Even more of a mystery, why doesn't He at least heal good, faithful servants who have faith that God will heal them?

Unfortunately, you won't find the answers to these questions in this book, but these issues, mysteries, and how to answer others who are asking these questions will be addressed. We understand it can be a bit intimidating to face a roomful of people, or even just one person, who asks "What is wrong with me that God will not heal me?" Even the most grounded believers can get nervous about the questions they may receive from attendees at a chronic illness support group. You may be thinking, "I know what I believe but I am not prepared to quote the Scriptures or explain exactly why I feel at peace about why God is not healing me."

Before my first radio interview about *Rest Ministries*, I sat at my computer with a headset and four pages of notes. I was to be broadcast 3000 miles away in Florida and I was trying not to be nervous. I knew what I was going to talk about and I could recite my verses, stories and statistics without notes. If the interviewer asked me why I believed I had not been healed, I could easily answer that God had shown me a path in which I could reach out to other people who were hurting and bring glory to Him.

The interview went fine, and then the host said, "Let's take a few calls." What!? I wasn't prepared for this! *Oh, please, God, don't let anyone get through that is going to ask me why God hasn't healed them.* I tried to prepare for this, just in case, but I couldn't find the answer. How could I tell someone "God may be glorified more through your illness than your health?" How cold! That wasn't the way to make friends. Who was I to claim I knew what God's will was for an individual? Thankfully, there was only time for a Christian doctor to request information before the program ended.

You are probably feeling the same way. "Who, me?! I don't know all of those verses about healing and I don't understand God's reasoning for suffering and pain." Those feelings that you are having are normal and, to be honest, I doubt I will ever find someone who truly can explain all the "whys" to me, because humans and God cannot be compared. Isaiah 55:8,9 says "Your thoughts are not my thoughts." Doesn't it stand to reason that God's logical explanation is not our logical explanation? Still, we must take a closer look and prepare, because just as the suffering will come, so too will the questions. This way, when we encounter them, we won't be surprised.

Unfortunately, none of these "answers" truly reveal the reason a person is going through a difficult time, but the next two chapters are a breakdown of some of the things that we do know about God and suffering.

Use this as your guide when you encounter the "whys?" Use it as a place to begin your understanding of God and suffering issues, but be aware that God doesn't reveal His purposes for every situation we will experience. David Beibel writes "Modern Christians sometimes rush to put His truth into little boxes, neatly systematized, categorized, and organized, and principalized, when God's perspective on suffering is too big for any of that. While for some, 'spirituality' is defined by what you know, for God it may be more how you handle what you *cannot* know."[1]

There are a lot of assumptions about healing:
- everyone who is a "good Christian" will be healed
- God wants everyone to be healed of physical ailments
- everyone who has an illness wants to be prayed over for healing
- those who have enough faith will be healed
- everyone should want to be healed
- saying "I will pray for you to be healed" is always the right thing to say
- reassuring someone, "I know God will heal you" is acceptable

This chapter includes a lot of first-person accounts, because healing is a very personal issue. Only by asking how people feel about healing and putting our assumptions aside can we begin to understand.

Healing is a personal issue

"There are some people in my small group who are able to see the subtle clues in my body language and face that I'm in pain, and who will ask me if I'd like to pray. They really ask me, not ask having already made up their mind what it is that I need for them to do." — Sherry

"Disabled people are healed in miracle stories," says Hurst, author of *Disability From the Point of View of Religion and Spirituality*. "These are often taken literally to mean that all disabled people should and would want to be healed in this way."[2] In John 5:6 Jesus asks a man who has been an invalid for thirty-eight years "Do you want to be healed?" Most of us may ask, "What kind of a question is that? Who would *not* want to be healed?"

Upon hearing many people's experiences about being prayed over for healing, there was one underlying theme: People want to be *asked*. This may come as a surprise to those who do not live with physical ailments, because the desire to be healed seems to be assumed. Over and over, people shared, however, that they resented people assuming that they wanted prayer for healing and that they appreciated people asking, "What would you like me to pray for?" Surely, Jesus understood this desire.

> "People have prayed for me for healing when I did not want it, and it has led me to feel uncomfortable with continued pain. I do not feel it is acceptable to remind people of this recurring need. I have also chosen to have prayer for healing from pain, because I felt the need, and the pain was relieved—as was the emotional distress I had been feeling." — Cheri

Throughout the Bible Jesus heals numerous people, but many of them came to Jesus asking for healing. When Jesus approached the man at the pools, the man may have even believed that Jesus was being sarcastic with him. "Who is this guy messing with me about healing? All I want to do is get into the pools, but people keep getting in front of me! Can he do something about that? Now *that* would be helpful!" The man had been an invalid for thirty-eight years, and when Jesus asked him "Do you want to get well?" the man didn't even answer Jesus' question, possibly believing that Jesus obviously didn't understand the circumstances. There are many different interpretations about why Jesus specifically asked the man if he wished to be healed.

Although we may know that God can heal us, when we live with illness or disability, we often feel that healing is a personal thing between ourselves and God. When people assume we want to be prayed for, despite their loving intentions, it can be interpreted as is a sign of disrespect. It makes those of us with illness feel foolish, as though we haven't considered that God can heal us with the swoop of His hand.

> "When I was recently in much constant pain and having months of sleepless nights due to pain and other things, I was put on the prayer list in the bulletin without my knowledge. At first, it bothered me. I usually keep this just within a few close friends so that I don't have to do a lot of explaining of the problem." —Ellie

This is a difficult thing for a church to understand. It should be standard practice, however, for anyone in leadership (or not) who is in a situation where a prayer for healing is believed to be desired, the person to be prayed over should be asked, "Would you like me/us to pray for your healing?" Or one can ask the person, "What would you like us to pray for?" Don't assume the answer is obvious. Many people will respond, "Please pray for my healing," and then one can be rest assured that the person feels comfortable asking God for healing.

Other people may respond to this question by saying, "Pray for God to give me the strength to get through this" or "Pray that I can accept God's will." To truly give the person comfort and peace, pray for what they ask you to pray for.

How do you pray for a person who doesn't request healing?
Here are some things that you can pray for:
- Say, "Lord, we don't even know what to ask for, but we know that You know our hearts."

- Ask God to bring the ill person comfort.
- Ask God to end or decrease the pain.
- Ask God to bless him with good rest and sleep.
- Ask God to give wisdom and discernment in the medical decisions that need to be made.
- Ask God to be with the ill person's family and loved ones who are worried.
- Ask God to be with the ill person's children who may be staying somewhere other than their own home.
- Ask God to give the doctors wisdom and discernment.
- Ask God to bring good caregivers/nurses into the person's environment.
- Ask God to send friends into the ill person's life.
- Ask God for effective medications with few side effects.

Bear in mind, the things that you pray for may not be what what one may typically expect. Last year when I was speaking to Claudette Palatsky, author of *Think It Not Strange,* she was due to have more tests done to try to discover the cause of her back pain. The pain was excruciating and yet occasionally it could subside to less intensity. I actually prayed that her pain would be at its *worst* on the day of her tests so that it represented what she actually was experiencing at home earlier in the week. Sometimes, when we have tests done, it can be extremely frustrating to go into the medical office and your body is having a better than typical day and it is not representative of the pain you are usually experiencing. After my prayer, Claudette, said that she had never had someone pray that she would actually *be* in pain, but that having her pain represented well during the tests *was* a concern and something that would definitely help her medical team to better be able to better locate the cause of the pain.

While it may seem odd to pray for someone to actually *be* in pain, you may find that if you live with chronic illness yourself, you have a deeper understanding of situations like this and be able to add a unique perspective in how you understand what they are experiencing. Your "inside knowledge" can be a gift that those who do not live with chronic illness have not been blessed with. So be sure to use it!

David Beibel shares this story in his book *How to Help a Heartbroken Friend*.

> "When Naomi was eighteen months old, spinal meningitis stole the hearing in her right ear. Three days after Christmas 1987, at forty-five years of age, she woke up to find herself totally deaf from the delayed effect of the same disease. What hindered her recovery most was not all the lifestyle adjustments required, though these were formidable enough, but 'those who insisted that by going to some healing service I would be miraculously healed — or the pastor -'friend' who wanted to pray for revelation of something in my past that was hindering my healing,' Naomi wrote. 'They looked on it as temporary testing by God and said we just needed to pray the right way. At the same time I was trying to accept the permanence of it. I do believe some are healed miraculously, but I felt I was not one of them, and to keep insisting that I go to some prayer meeting so they could pray for me was hindering the grief process. They were not accepting what I was trying accept."[3]

Prayer for healing should never overshadow a relationship with Christ

It is easy to get caught up in all of the scriptures where Jesus heals those who are ill and actually taking our focus off of God and who He is. Our time of fellowship with Him should not be one made up of negotiating about what we will do if we are healed and promises on how we will use it to glorify Him.

Since the beginning of my induction into the world of chronic illness ministry, I have seen many people who spend the majority of their time focusing strictly on the healing that they are positive is to come as they join into a treasure hunt searching for what they believe is the secret formula in order for God to work His magic of healing. Unfortunately, their actual relationship with the Lord falters, as their focus in life no longer revolves around a relationship with God, but rather, a search for how they can maintain the right behavior in order to have God reward them with a healthy body. You may recall reading Rest Ministries viewpoint on healing in an earlier chapter. The part about this states:

> We caution against worshipping "the idea of healing" rather than God, (Exodus 20:3). Although we encourage people to pray for God's healing, we also comfort them in their pain; as we believe that we are called to comfort others in their pain, as God has comforted us in our own (2 Corinthians 1:3-5), even when we are still living with pain in our own lives (1 Peter 4:10).

Ed Dobson, a pastor who lives with the disease ALS (Lou Gehrig's disease) and is the author of *Prayers and Promises When Facing a Life-Threatening Illness,* describes the advice he received about keeping the priority of healing in the right perspective:

"Before Wayne annoited me with oil he gave me this advice: 'Do not become obsessed with healing. Get lost in the wonder of God, and who knows what God will do for you.' Get lost in the wonder of God. I have been lost in the wonder of my disease. Now I was being told to get lost in the wonder of God. So I have tried to lift my focus off of my disease and keep it connected to the wonder of God."[4]

Prayer for healing should not be done out of obligation

"I was healed of two incurable illnesses, but it does not seem to be in God's plan at present to heal me of chronic fatigue syndrome. I've been in prayer groups where you felt an obligation, and I resented that immensely." — Virginia

We all have a great desire to see our friends and family well. Who of us wants to see someone we love suffer? Circumstances are rarely in our control, however, and as Christians, what is the first thing we tend to do when things are beyond our control? We pray about it! We pray that God will right the wrongs, correct the crooked, and heal the sick. It's easy to get caught up in the excitement of seeing God work.

"I think the worst thing is when people want to pray for complete healing of my pain and/or disability. Sometimes I get the impression that if this doesn't happen they feel something is wrong with me or their prayer. That it's not okay to be in pain or to suffer, not really and truly. That God would never want us to continue to be in pain . . . which is, of course, not what God says in the Bible at all!" —Cherie

Enthusiasm about healing is not always contagious, and healthy people can't understand why an ill person isn't excited about the potential to see God work in his or her life. We insist on praying for them. We insist on sprinkling oil on their head, and we impatiently wait for God to "zap 'em!" We want to hear God first hand say "Pick up your mat and walk," (John 5:11), "Take off the grave clothes and let him go," (John 11:44), "Woman, you are set free from your infirmity," (Luke 13:12). We may get so over zealous about the healing, however, that we forget about the person.

> "I have been prayed for several times. Finally, I asked Him myself and I heard a resounding, 'no.' It's time to move on and somehow make this a positive experience." —Rebecca

There are a variety of reasons why an ill person may not wish to have someone pray for her healing. Some of these are positive, acceptable reasons. Others are understandable, but not spiritually correct. Either way, a person should *never* be forced, coherced, or obligated to be prayed over. You can always pray silently; God hears us regardless.

Some of the positive reasons may include:
- She feels like God is blessing her through the illness
- She has come to view the world differently since she was diagnosed
- She has come to know God on a deeper level because of her illness
- She may worry about what would happen to her faith if she didn't have to depend on God as much as she does now while living with this illness
- She is seeing God work through her illness and use it to help other people

There are a wide variety of ways that churches go about praying for healing. Some have altar calls or revivals. Others have the ill person come to the church office and quietly be prayed for by the elders. Regardless of how your church does it, it is important that the ill person and their comfort zone be respected. A church or leaders within the church should never insist on praying for someone out loud if the person does not want to be prayed for (and if she is asked, you will kno.!) If the person feels uncomfortable, the church risks that person never returning or returning, but never feeling comfortable in that church again.

> "Rosalie visits a church for the first time. Because she is deaf, but can do pretty well with her hearing aids, she sits in the front. When the healing service begins, she is asked to come forward. Feeling pressured, she does. The minister prays loudly, covers her ears, and asks the Lord to heal her. She is stunned, but wants to be polite. The next week, when she visits the church again, she leaves her hearing aids off. Now Rosalie can understand almost nothing, but she does not want to disappoint all of the people who prayed for her."[5]

Some of the understandable, but spiritually incorrect reasons a person does not want anyone to pray for their healing may include:

- She doesn't believe that God is concerned enough about her to heal her
- She doesn't think that she has enough faith in God to be healed
- She thinks that the illness is her punishment and she deserves it
- She believes that she has committed too many sins to ask for God to heal her

If one feels these are the reasons that a person refuses prayer for healing, then a minister or even a good friend should counsel this person on what it means to be a Christian. The person may need to be led into accepting Jesus

Christ, asking for forgiveness, and understanding God's grace. Under these circumstances, however, it is important that the person understand that healing is not guaranteed just because she has become a Christian. Whether one is healed or not is not dependent on good works, the amount of faith, or sin which has been confessed. She will likely have many questions, and a chronic illness/pain small group would be a good place for her to gain insight and emotional support.

Lack of healing does not necessarily signify a hidden sin

> "When I was at an intercessory prayer meeting to pray for the church, everyone decided to pray for me. They tried to get me to confess my 'hidden sin,' saying that I was hiding something. After six years of suffering with a terminal illness, I had and have confessed all that I know as sin, and I have come to realize that His grace is sufficient for me. I am hiding no 'hidden sin.' I am very transparent and can honestly say that there is not one day that goes by where my holiness will ever stack up. I am either saved by the blood of Jesus or I am not." — Jenny

When Jesus heard that his good friend Lazarus was ill, He responded by saying, "This sickness will not end in death. No, it is for God's glory so that God's Son may be glorified through it," (John 11:4). Jesus didn't say, "He is ill because of sin." There are instances in the Bible where a warning is given. When Jesus healed the man by the pools He then told him, "Stop sinning or something worse may happen to you," (John 5:14). The man *did* have sin in his life, but Jesus chose to approach the man and offer him healing despite the sin.

From this, can we assume that not all illness is a result of sin? And even if there is sin, Jesus still has the option to heal us in spite of it. When a person prays for healing and is not healed, oftentimes the people around him will quickly assume that the person has sin in his life and that is why God has refused to heal. It makes sense. It is logical. This way, God is understandable to us. We who do not live with physical limitations can rest easy that nothing will happen to us since we are obeying God.

God doesn't work this way. As mentioned earlier, his ways are different that our ways. We cannot comprehend how He chooses to make decisions. When we try to package him into a box and say, "'A' plus 'B', must equal 'C,'" we are limiting the greatest power and making judgements where we have no knowledge. God tells us in Isaiah 55:8-9, "For My thoughts are not your thoughts, neither are your ways My ways. As the heavens are higher than the earth, so are My ways higher than your ways and My thoughts than your thoughts."

Lack of healing does not necessarily signify a lack of faith

"Rise and go. Your faith has made you well," (Luke 17:19). There are various incidents throughout the Bible where the Word refers to one being healed because of his or her faith. When a woman approached Jesus, sure that by just touching His clothing she would be cured her from her sickness, Jesus responded by saying, "Daughter, your faith has healed you. Go in peace and be freed from your suffering."

Does this mean that when one is not healed it is because of a lack of his or her faith? Oftentimes, when healing does not occur people are quick to say, "You weren't healed because you did not have enough faith." Is all healing dependent on faith?

> "We don't know the hearts of those who aren't healed, only God does. But oftentimes I've seen people who weren't healed under condemnation when the pain

doesn't lift. There is truth involved with a lot of damaging condemnation. This is hurtful and painful to hear." —Kathy

If you have not yet been told by someone that your lack of healing is due to your lack of faith or possibly sin in your life, consider yourself the minority. When I was first diagnosed with rheumatoid arthritis there were many well-meaning people who wanted me to continually ask for forgiveness to get rid of that sin that was, in their opinion, causing this disease to take over my body. It was emotionally painful, and so I turned to Joni Earickson Tada to see how she handled these kind of comments. After all, as Martin Luther once said, "They gave our Master a crown of thorns. Why do we hope for a crown of roses?"

Joni states on her website the following response to people who tell her "If you have enough faith you would be able to walk."

> "First, faith comes from hearing the word of God (Romans 10:17) and if you spend any time in God's word, you'll see that He related to suffering in many more ways than to heal it. Time and again, God shows us that suffering refines our faith (1 Peter 1:7), builds character (Romans 8:28), and draws us closer to Christ, to name a few for 'To this [suffering] you were called, because Christ suffered for you, leaving you an example that you should follow in His steps' (1 Peter 2:21). Healing is an earthly fix . . . I'm looking for the long term benefits which hardship will gain me in heaven for 'those who suffer with Him, we shall reign with Him' (2 Timothy 2:12). I want what God wants; if it's living in a wheelchair, fine; if it's being healed, that's fine too. I've learned to be content in plenty or in want."[6]

According to Mark 6:5,6, it is possible to be healed even when there is a lack of faith present. "He (Jesus) could not do any miracles there, except lay his hands on a few sick people and heal them. And He was amazed at their lack of faith."

These people in Jesus' hometown lacked faith — so much so that even Jesus was *amazed* (and we're not talking "amazed" in a positive sense here). Yet, He chose to have compassion on them and heal them anyway. Who are we to judge why a person has not been healed? Only our Lord can truly know why He has not chosen (or has chosen) to heal a person.

> "At my church, I have been meeting with a prayer counselor, in this case the Minister of Counseling and her prayer partner. They 'soak' me in prayer. It is a time of being ministered by the spirit and a reminder that God is holding us, even through this illness. We also ask for healing, if it is in God's sovereign will. It is a wonderful time for myself, and I was able to speak of the small group, which do not attend our church, and iron out those issues. If needed, my husband comes with me and receives prayer too!" — Kathy

It should also be noted that each individual's medical choices should be respected. Taking medication does not mean that a person lacks faith. God is the great physician, but He also has equipped human physicians with knowledge and skills. Willie says, "I still take pain medications, and I was *chastised* by the church at one point for my lack of faith." In my opinion, yhis is unfortunate as well as incorrect theology.

God does physically heal us . . . sometimes

God can and does heal people every day. Let us not forget this fact and praise Him for it. Who and when He chooses to heal cannot be predicted. Healing comes in many forms . . . and sometimes that is a physical healing of all of our symptoms, or perhaps just some of them.

"I had hypoglycemia and had been on a strict diet for over nine months. At a Bible study, one of the little old ladies had prepared cinnamon rolls. She was very upset that I couldn't eat them and said 'God can take care of that' laid her little hands on me and prayed a simple prayer and I was surprised to find that I was indeed healed! It had not one thing to do with my faith, for sure! I guess maybe God liked the lady's cinnamon rolls! I suspect God really liked that little old lady, who is now with Him. Another time, I had been diagnosed with rheumatoid arthritis and was really suffering in my knees. I attended a healing mission at church and was surprised to be called out as one who had recently gotten that diagnosis. Only one person there knew I'd had that diagnosis and she was not a member of the church. Yes, I was healed and the evidence was I could kneel to pray which I had not been able to do in months. I believe there are lessons to be learned in some illness that I might not learn otherwise. I would like to be healed of chronic fatigue syndrome and to have energy, but until that happens, I pray that God helps me learn, and I lift up the pain and weakness for the salvation of others. Maybe my prayers at those times will help others in some way. In some ways, that helps relieve the guilt and loss that I feel, because a lot of the time my concentration is so bad that I cannot pray." — Virginia

God heals in many ways—not just physically

"I have pulled through more crises and troubles than I can tell. I think my biggest miracle of all was the emotional healing I received from the Lord. I was a Spirit-filled Christian and ministering full-time when I became seriously sick. I then went through a wilderness period that was most unbearable. After my twenty-eighth hospitalization I wanted to give up. Emotionally and spiritually I was dead. God healed me. I now know His grace. I now have peace and joy, depression is hardly ever a problem. I know more of His Word than ever. I have learned to keep my shield up from the condemnation attacks. I love to minister God's grace to chronically sick people.

The emotional realm always needs healing and in this area I see dramatic results. I have witnessed miracles of healing — amazing things — and I know God heals. But for every one of those I see over a thousand who are not physically healed. I do know that emotional healing can be almost one-hundred percent when one ministers compassion and grace to the individual freeing them from condemnation. When a physically ill person is set free in their soul and spirit, they experience less pain physically. I know that as fact because I have experienced it." — Jenny

The late Tim Hansel wrote in his book *You Gotta Keep Dancin'*:

"I have prayed hundreds, if not thousands, of times for the Lord to heal me — and He finally healed me of the need to be healed. I had discovered a peace inside the pain. I finally came to the realization that if the Lord could use this body better the way it is, then that's the way it should be. I'm quite sure I would be a different person were it not for my accident."[7]

I asked other people to also share with me some of their healing experiences.

"I have been to many healing services and have been prayed over many times. I believe that God has touched me in some way, but I have not received the physical healing that I personally would wish for. I also believe that suffering has a purpose and is not necessarily something to run from (although my human nature wants to), but rather something to embrace for Jesus' sake if it happens to exist. If a healing is to occur it must be for His glory, not just to make our lives easier. Maybe some of us suffer so that others can practice their Christian charity on us? It is difficult to accept this help many times, but then that helps us to grow in humility. I don't know the answer here, but would encourage anyone with chronic pain to be prayed over as often as the opportunity presents itself. We don't always see any visible results, as a matter of fact, most times we don't, but prayer is never wasted. Never cease to pray for healing, but realize that in the end it is God's will, not ours. In some way our suffering is a help to our souls, if not God would not allow it." —Janine

"I love the Lord Jesus Christ with all of my heart and soul, and I know that He could heal me in a moment if He wanted to. He could provide the cures for diabetes, cancer, aids, lupus, or any other diseases if He so chose. I also believe that He uses all things (good or bad) for His purposes and for His glory. People just don't understand unless they too have experienced a disability." —Donna

Healing is a complicated issue, and there are so many strong opinions regarding it. Many books have been written on the subject, and even they seem somewhat incomplete. This is definitely an area where greater understanding is needed by all individuals.

"I believe churches need to teach on healing and what happens when it doesn't come. There are many controversial points on healing. I had a small group of people call me and want me to attend a healing school. The idea is to 'speak the word' and constantly be running scripture through your head day and night, claiming God's Word. The more seed (God's Word) you receive in you, be prepared for more pain, because

Satan attacks you then even more, and You have to fight the battle. I just wasn't sure about this." —Kathy

One of the best books on this topic I believe is *Will God Heal Me?: God's Power and Purpose in Suffering* by Ron Dunn. He describes what to do when healing does not come.

> "If we are still not healed after having done all we know to do, the next step is to accept our afflictions as part of God's ongoing ministry in us. To God, character is far more precious than comfort. He often uses uncomfortable circumstances to change our character. When the circumstances have fulfilled their task, then God may change the circumstances. But if He doesn't, it'll be all right because our character will have been so changed that we will be able to live with uncomfortable circumstances. Paul's own thorn-in-the-flesh experience is a perfect example of changed character rejoicing in the midst of changed circumstances."[8]

In leading a small group for those with chronic illness, you must admit you will not have all the answers. You will not understand why some members are healed and others are not. You will not comprehend why some members are diagnosed with one illness after another, and sometimes even their family members, who are caregivers, are then are diagnosed with illnesses such as cancer. Or why does God heal a person to have them suffer from a car accident a week later?

There is no logical way for us to explain suffering. Although our troubled thoughts prompt us to answer because we are greatly disturbed (Job 20:2), the Lord knows the thoughts of man; He knows that they are futile (Psalm 94:11). However, we do know that God does have our best interests at heart (Jeremiah 29:11). I hope this chapter and the following chapter will give you an overview of the issue of healing as well as our call to suffer, so that you feel you have some general knowledge to at least explain your opinion on healing and suffering when members in your group bring it up.

"Sympathy is a shallow stream in the souls of those who have not suffered."
William E. Sangster

"It is a fact of Christian experience that life is a series of troughs and peaks. In His efforts to get permanent possession of a soul, God relies on the troughs more than the peaks. And some of His special favorites have gone through longer and deeper troughs than anyone else."
Peter Marshall

"The truth that many people never understand, until it is too late, is that the more you try to avoid suffering the more you suffer, because smaller things begin to torture you in proportion to your fear of suffering."
Thomas Merton

"One thing we may be sure of, however: For the believer all pain has meaning; all adversity is profitable. There is no question that adversity is difficult. It usually takes us by surprise and seems to strike where we are most vulnerable. To us it often appears completely senseless and irrational, but to God none of it is either senseless or irrational. He has a purpose in every pain He brings or allows in our lives. We can be sure that in some way He intends it for our profit and His glory."
Jerry Bridge

"Pain is a kindly, hopeful thing, a certain proof of life, a clear assurance that all is not yet over, that there is still a chance."
Arthur John (A. J.) Gossip

CHAPTER 17

Answering tough questions: Why must we suffer?

One of the greatest mysteries of our God is why He allows people to suffer and how He goes about choosing or allowing who will experience what form of suffering. Let's take a closer look at suffering. I am not an expert on the theology of suffering, but I hope that the highlights on this topic that I have provided will be a starting place to help you put your beliefs into words if people ask you to explain your them.

Why does God let bad things happen?

Some people may argue that the fact that there are good people who suffer proves that God is either not all-powerful or not all-good. Either way, they believe the Bible contradicts itself by claiming that God is both good and powerful. When we witness tragedy and unfairness we have the choice to either (1) deny that God is a personal God, concerned with our circumstances; (2) believe that God is good, but some things are beyond His control (as concluded by Rabbi Kishner in *Why Bad Things Happen To Good People);* or (3) believe that "whatever will be will be!" It must be God's will.

Here are some scriptures for you to read to better understand the character of God:

- God is pleased with those who do good, and slowly angers with those who resist Him. (Psalm 7:11; Nahum 1:1-7).
- God feels grief toward those who reject Him (Genesis 6:6; Psalm 95:10).
- God hurts when He must correct and punish us for our own good (Isaiah 63:9).
- God finds no pleasure in judging the wicked, and He hopes they will change their heart (Ezekial 18:23,32; 33:11).
- God finds delight in kindness, justice, and righteousness (Jeremiah 9:24).
- God loved the world so much that he became a part of humanity, in the form of Jesus Christ, and died like a sinner so that we could be saved (John 3:16; 2 Corinthians 5:21).

Did God give me this illness or allow it?

This is a point of contention among many people and you will get no particular right or wrong answer. In your group of six people, you may end up with six viewpoints or at the least a strong two. In my book *Why Can't I Make People Understand? Discovering the Validation Those with Chronic Illness Seek and Why,* I explain my own personal belief about my illness.

> "Many people feel, 'God gave me this illness.' Others take great offense at this viewpoint and claim that illness is the result of living in a sinful world and God simply allowed it. Personally, I look to Luke 14:27: 'Anyone who does not carry his cross and follow Me cannot be My disciple.' My illness is a cross that I choose to accept to carry. Regardless of what you believe, join me in clinging to Romans 11:36: 'For from Him and through Him and to Him are all things. To Him be the glory forever! Amen.' Whatever the reason

for this cross we are asked to carry, God was involved in the decision-making process 100 percent. But you are responsible for making sure that it glorifies God. Imagine for a moment a large cross sitting in your backyard leaning up against the house. Go on out there with a wood-burning kit and burn in the name of your illness. This is your cross. It may be temporary or it may be permanent, but you can choose to throw tar and feathers at it or get out some decoupage and see what God is going to make out of it. By carrying your cross, you are a disciple. Welcome to the family.[1]

I particularly like how Charles Spurgeon explains his belief about the purpose for his depression:

"It would be a very sharp and trying experience to me to think that I have an affliction which God never sent me, that the bitter cup was never filled by His hand, that my trials were never measured out by Him nor sent to me by His arrangement of their weight and quantity. . . . He who made no mistakes in balancing the clouds and meting out the heavens, commits no errors in measuring out the ingredients which compose the medicine of souls."[2]

Here are some things we *do* know:

- **God is in control of history.** Paul declared that "He has made from one blood every nation of men to dwell on all the face of the earth, and has determined their preappointed times and the boundaries of their dwellings," (Acts 17:26).
- **God is active in history even when it seems He is not.** For example, more than thirty years after being the victim of his brothers' hatred, Joseph told them "Do not be afraid, for am I in the place of God. But as for you, you meant evil against me; but God meant it

for good, in order to bring it about as it is this day, to save many people alive," (Genesis 50:19-20).

- **One may not easily be able to tell which part of history was God's doing and which was not since His actions are so interwoven with earthly and human factors.** We do know that He is a holy God who hates sin, therefore, He is never responsible for leading anyone to do evil. He can, however, work through our own human sin to accomplish His purposes.

Why does God allow sickness and disease?

We recognize that suffering can help us grow spiritually, (Hebrews 12:6) and yet some of the afflictions in life seem cruel and useless. If a baby is born with a deformity, who benefits? When a giving, caring, loving person is diagnosed with an illness, it doesn't seem fair. Oftentimes, it is hard for us to see the purpose behind the suffering that we encounter.

To explain God's purpose in suffering I look towards one of the people I admire most who speaks on this topic frequently, Joni Eareckson Tada. On her web page at www.joniandfriends.com she is asked, "What is your response to people who ask, 'Why is God doing this to me?'" she answers,

"First, God's decrees allow for suffering to happen, but He doesn't 'do' it; He doesn't say 'Into each life a little rain must fall,' and then turn the 'hose' in earth's general direction to see who gets the wettest. He screens every trial, filtering our hardships through His hands, and allowing only certain afflictions to touch us – afflictions which are in complete keeping with His perfect will in our lives. I realize this is hard to swallow for many Christians, but think of the alternative. Think if God didn't control suffering. Our lives would be much worse – absolutely intolerable – every moment of the day. If God didn't control suffering, suffering would come at us uncontrolled. I don't want to live in a world like that! I'd rather take things from the 'left hand of God' than no hand at all! In short, He permits what He hates to accomplish what He loves. And what does He love? Christ in us, the hope of glory."[3]

Here are some main points to keep in mind.

There is a reason for each affliction, even though we cannot see it

Jesus said that a man was born blind "that the works of God should be revealed in him," (John 9:3). Then Jesus healed the man. Up until this point, no one knew why the man had been blind, but God did. That was all that mattered. Sometimes, we must rest in the assurance that God knows the answer to the "why?" even when we do not.

We were never promised a perfect life here on earth

Peter tells us in 1 Peter 4:12, "Dear friends, do not be surprised at the painful trial you are suffering, as though something strange were happening to you." Suffering is a direct result of sin's entrance into the world. Oftentimes, our troubles may be the side-effects of the sin that has entered our world, even though it is no fault of our own. In the New Testament, the apostle Paul described the whole creation of God as groaning and eagerly anticipating the time when it will be freed from the curse of decay and be remade, free from the effects of sin (Romans 8:19-22). We may all intellectually realize that God has are best interests at heart and that does not include indefinite comfort, but we can also relate to something C.S. Lewis once said: "We're not necessarily doubting that God will do the best for us; we are wondering how painful the best will turn out to be."

Suffering is inevitable

Joni Eareckson Tada shares in her extraordinary book, *When God Weeps: Why Our Sufferings Matter to the Almighty*, how we are sometimes quick to adapt scripture's meaning to best fit our own desires for comfort.

Mark 1:32-39 says, "When evening came, after the sun had set, they began bringing to Him all who were ill and those who were demon-possessed. And the whole city had gathered at the door. And He healed many who were ill with various diseases, and cast out many demons; and He was not permitting the demons to speak, because they knew who He was. In the early morning, while it was still dark, Jesus got up, left the house, and went away to a secluded place, and was praying there. And His companions searched for Him; they found Him, and said to Him, 'Everyone is looking for You.' He said to them, 'Let us go somewhere else to the towns nearby, so that I may preach there also; for that is what I came for.'"

Joni shares, "'So I can *preach*,' He says. '*That* is why I have come.' Not that He didn't care about the cancer-ridden and feverish in Capernaum who had gotten word too late to come for healing the night before. But their illnesses weren't His focus—the Gospel was. His miracles were a backdrop, a visual aid, to His urgent message. That message was: Sin will kill you, hell is real, God is merciful, His kingdom will change you, I am your passport. Whenever people missed this point—whenever the immediate benefit of His miracles distracted them from eternal things—the Savior backed away." (See John 6:26, 27)[4]

Suffering can be caused by the results our choices

Since God made us able to make free choices, we have made and will continue to make less than ideal or safe decisions. We may take risks. My hand surgeon typically does surgery on professional athletes and he has said, "I tell these other patients of mine, you know, there is this woman with rheumatoid arthritis that takes whatever comes at her. She isn't snowboarding down a mountain and getting hurt and then expecting me to fix her back up so she can go out there and do it again. She just wants to hold a cup of coffee."

Suffering may be a product of Satan

Job's life story is a vivid example of how a good person can suffer incredible tragedy because of satanic attack. God allowed Satan to take away Job's possessions, his family, and his health (Job 1,2). Job was a living testimonial to the trustworthiness of God. He illustrated that a person can trust God and maintain integrity even when one's life falls apart, because God is worth trusting. In the end, Job learned that even though he didn't understand what God was up to, he had plenty of reason to believe that God was not being unjust, cruel, or unfair by allowing things in his life to crumble (Job 42).

The apostle Paul experienced a physical problem that he attributed to Satan. He called it a "thorn in the flesh... , a messenger of Satan to buffet me," (2 Corinthians 12:7). Paul prayed to have the thorn taken away, but God did not answer that prayer. Instead, He helped Paul to see how the difficulty could serve a good purpose. This weakness made Paul humbly dependent on God and put him in a position to experience God's grace (vv. 8-10). [Although most cases of sickness cannot be directly tied to Satan's work, the gospel accounts do record a few examples of suffering attributed to Satan, including a blind and mute man (Matthew 12:22) and a boy who suffered seizures (17:14-18).]

God sometimes uses suffering to get our attention

Some people turn away from God when they face difficulties, but for a number of people the suffering brings them into a closer relationship with God. Says Karen, a woman with lupus, "I decided that, regardless of my circumstances, I would much rather have God beside me than live my life without Him." Jack Graham says, "Sometimes God has to put us flat on our back before we are looking up to Him." Paul wrote similar things about his physical troubles. The Lord told Paul, "My grace is sufficient for you, for My strength is made perfect in weakness," (2 Corinthians 12:9). Then Paul added, "Therefore I take pleasure in infirmities, in reproaches, in needs, in persecutions, in distresses, for Christ's sake. For when I am weak, then I am strong," (v. 10).

Suffering forces us to evaluate the direction of our lives

We can choose to despair by focusing on our present problems, or we can choose to hope by recognizing God's long-range plan for us (Romans 5:5; 8:18, 28; Hebrews 11). Suffering makes us recognize how weak the things that we put our faith in really are. Our finances, our jobs, our health, our loved ones, can all be taken away, and then what are we to depend on? By suffering, we are forced to reevaluate our priorities, values, goals, dreams, pleasures, the source of real strength, and our relationships with people and with God. If we don't turn away from God, it is bound to bring us into a closer relationship with God.

God suffers with us and is beside us in our darkest times

Scripture assures us that He won't allow us to have more than we can handle. Isaac Newton once said, "Trials are medicines which our gracious and wise Physician prescribes because we need them; and he proportions the frequency and weight of them to what the case requires. Let us trust his skill and thank him for his prescription." Hebrews 13:5b says, "Never will I leave you; never will I forsake you."

Suffering puts us in the position where we need to be with other believers

Paul uses the analogy of a human body (1 Corinthians 12) to explain our need of other believers in order to function properly. "And if one member suffers, all the members suffer with it; or if one member is honored, all the members rejoice with it. Now you are the body of Christ, and members individually," (vv. 26,27). In the New Testament the phrase, "one another" is used more than fifty times to describe our relationship with other believers. God tells us to encourage one another, love one another, accept one another, bear one another's burdens, build one another up, and of course, pray for one another. "God didn't create us to be involved in a solo sport," someone once said. "Christianity is a team sport. Personal involvement with other believers fosters spiritual growth by providing an environment of intimacy, encouragement and accountability."[5]

Suffering puts us in the position to bring comfort to others when they must suffer

In 2 Corinthians 1, Paul writes, "Blessed be the God and Father of our Lord Jesus Christ, the Father of mercies and God of all comfort, who comforts us in all our tribulation, that we may be able to comfort those who are in any trouble, with the comfort with which we ourselves are comforted by God," (vv. 3,4). In *Where Is God When It Hurts?*, author Philip Yancey writes about Joni Eareckson Tada, "She wrestled with God, yes, but she did not turn away from Him. . . Joni now calls her accident a 'glorious intruder,' and claims it was the best thing that ever happened to her. God used it to get her attention and direct her thoughts toward Him."[6] And through Joni's own story, she has been influential in bringing millions of people to know about Jesus.

We cry out for complete answers. We feel abandoned in our suffering. Even Jesus Christ himself felt this way as He was hanging on the cross and cried out "My God! Why have you forsaken me?" We are not alone in our search for an explanation of our pain. Rather than give us an answer, God offers Himself to us instead. Through experience we learn that just knowing God is enough in order for us to live. If we know that we can trust Him, we don't need full explanations. We need to just rest in the peace that our pain and suffering are not meaningless. It's enough to know that God still rules the universe and that He really does care about us as individuals.

John 14:27 says "The peace I give isn't like the peace the world gives. So don't be troubled or afraid." Just as we experience suffering that we do not understand, so too can we experience peace that is beyond human comprehension.

Yancey explains in *Where is God When it Hurts?* that the Bible doesn't always have an answer to our 'whys.'

> "The Bible consistently changes the questions we bring to the problem of pain. It rarely, or ambiguously, answers the backward-looking question 'Why?' Instead, it raises the very different, forward-looking question, 'To what end?' We are not put on earth merely to satisfy our desires, to pursue life, liberty and happiness. We are here to be changed, to be made more like God in order to prepare us for a lifetime with him. And that process may be served by the mysterious pattern of all creation: pleasure sometimes emerges against a background of pain, evil may be transformed into good, and suffering may produce something of value."[7]

When we begin to feel that God lacks concern about our pain, we need only look at the gift God gave us in sacrificing His son, Jesus Christ. God loved our suffering world so much that He sent His Son to agonize and die for us, to free us from being sentenced to eternal sorrow (John 3:16-18). Because Jesus died for us, we will never have to face the worst pain of all—total separation from God. Because of Christ, we can endure even the worst of tragedies now because of the strength He gives us and the hope for a better world.

People will come to you asking "Why me? Why this? Why now?" The best thing to do is to be truthful with them and tell them you don't know. They will appreciate your honesty. Lead them through some of the keypoints that this chapter has listed and reassure them that you will be beside them on their illness journey, even when you don't know all of the answers. David Biebel writes in his book *If God Is So Good, Why Do I Hurt So Bad?*, "Perhaps even more profound may be the conclusion that your faith will be stronger if you can't understand than if you do."[8]

*"God uses suffering to purge sin from our lives,
strengthen our commitment to Him, force us to depend
on grace, bind us together with other believers, produce
discernment, foster sensitivity, discipline our minds,
spend our time wisely, stretch our hope, cause us to know
Christ better, make us long for truth, lead us to
repentance of sin, teach us to give thanks in time of
sorrow, increase faith, and strengthen character."*
Joni Eareckson Tada

*"I learned a long time ago . . . that folks who are
trying to be kind would rather do it with a
macaroni-and-cheese bake than any personal
involvement. You hand off a serving dish and
you've done your job—no need to get personally
involved, and your conscience is clean. Food is the
currency of aid. . . if they truly wanted to be saviors,
they'd call the insurance company and spend four hours
on the phone arguing over bills, so I wouldn't have to."*
Jodi Picoult, Handle with Care: A Novel

*"Joy is not the absence of suffering.
It is the presence of God."*
Robert Schuller

*"A good friend is a connection to life –
a tie to the past, a road to the future,
the key to sanity in a totally insane world."*
Lois Wyse

CHAPTER 18
BEYOND SMALL GROUPS

How a church can make a significant difference

When you first picked up this book and started to read, you may have thought that chronic illness/pain ministry was as simple as providing an encouraging place for people with illness to comfort and uplift one another. As you read through this book, however, you probably realized just how many factors there are when in comes to the spiritual community and living with chronic pain. You may be thinking, "I never knew there were so many assumptions about illness, healing, and how to minister to someone with a chronic illness. How can I help? How can I make more people understand?"

Churches are already overwhelmed with obvious needs in other areas of ministry. So if people aren't saying anything about their physical pain, it becomes easy for the church to forget the daily needs of the chronically ill and assume that they are coping with the situation just fine. It's presumed their faith and the ability to pray for strength should be enough.

In Luke 14:21 Jesus shares a parable of a great banquet. When the host's friends all turned down his hospitality he commands, "Go out quickly into the streets and alleys of the town and bring in the poor, the crippled, the blind and the lame." This is still a mandate to us today, but we must remember that to provide a place where we offer hospitality, we must first "go out" into our own pews and provide a place of refuge; then these people who have experienced the comfort in your church will be there to bring in the wounded from the community and walk alongside them.

While this book's primary focus has been on starting a small group, you have likely thought of many ways that those with chronic illness and the church body could work together to improve communication and form a tighter knit community.

Chronic illness ministry is much more than gathering a group of people in a room and debating about why God has allowed them to have an illness. Chronic illness ministry is more than someone in the church asking an ill person, "How are you feeling?" Chronic illness ministry involves a change in awareness, attitude and actions. It involves knowing what people who live with illness would like from their church — and how to give *to* their church — and then work to establish ministries that will meet those needs.

In *The Message*, Proverbs 3:27 says, "Never walk away from someone who deserves help; your hand is God's hand for that person. Don't tell your neighbor 'Maybe some other time' or 'Try me tomorrow' when the money's right there in your pocket. Don't figure ways of taking advantage of your neighbor when he's sitting there trusting and unsuspecting."

Whether your church leadership acknowledges it or not, the church body has many ailing bodies, and they are often accompanied by broken spirits.

Blair and Blair says, "The religious system that permits its spiritual guides to remain ignorant about the place of those who are differently-abled in God's world must eventually question the depth of its own and its members' commitment to God's service."[1] We are commanded to not allow situations like this to occur:

"My reason for going back to church after many years away was to find supportive people who I thought would be understanding. After choir rehearsals, we always ask for prayer requests. I have asked for help to endure the constant pain I am in. There has only been one woman (who has lupus) who has ever asked me how I was feeling or if she could help in any way. Most just see my 'apparent' healthy smile and assume I am perfectly well. I don't expect people to fuss over me or make a big issue; I just wish for someone to talk to when I have really bad days. I had hoped Christian people would be more sensitive to the needs of people in pain. Maybe if there was more information and ways of letting concerned people know how to help, people like myself could be more open and discuss things with others." — Lynette

Ways to be sensitive to those with chronic or invisible illnesses

Those who do not have a chronic illness may wonder, "Why do I have to be so careful about what to say around people with illness? Aren't they being a little too sensitive?" Well . . . yes and no.

According to Rev. Dale Robbins, studies have shown that a great percentage of persons who cease attending church do so because of some type of offense or injury to their *feelings* that happened in church. Robbins says, "Other times, people are themselves at fault for being too touchy or sensitive to misunderstandings."[2]

Sometimes we are just uninforned and we don't realize that we are saying something that could be hurtful. Then there are those times when we are vaguely aware that we are using sarcasm as a form of passive aggression, we are tired of "sick people always being so needy; somebody needs to tell them to get over it and quit looking for free help." We all have moments of sinful attitudes, and even if you live with chronic illness yourself, you've likely felt tired of illness and all that the daily regime entails.

Yancey writes in his book, *Where is God When it Hurts?*,

> "I have interviewed many Christians with life-threatening illnesses, and every one without exception, has told me how damaging it can be to have a visitor plant the thought 'You must have done something to deserve this punishment.' At the very moment when they most need hope and strength to battle the illness, they get instead a frosty dose of guilt and self-doubt."[3]

We are to humble ourselves. We must remember that we are made in the image of Christ. Philippians 2:2-4 says, "Then make my joy complete by being like-minded, having the same love, being one in spirit and purpose. Do nothing out of selfish ambition or vain conceit, but in humility consider others better than yourselves. Each of you should look not only to your own interests, but also to the interests of others."

It's important to be aware of what others are going through and their interests, because we are their siblings in Christ. Knowing how to make a person feel loved and cared for should be at the top of our priorities.

We are to be wise, looking for opportunities to respond as Jesus would. "Be *wise* in the way that you act toward *outsiders*; make the most of every opportunity. Let your *conversation* be always full of grace, seasoned with salt, so that you may *know how to answer everyone*" (Colossians 4:4-6). It is vital that when we speak to both Christians and non-Christians we represent our Savior in a way with which He would be pleased.

We are to not speak of situations we have not experienced. It's important that we be careful to not give our opinion about things that we know little or nothing about.

Philip Yancey, author of *Where is God When it Hurts?* writes, "Perhaps the most unsettling aspect of the book [of Job] is that the arguments of Job's friend sound suspiciously like those offered by Christians today . . . .God dismissed all of Jobs' friends' high-sounding theories with a scowl. 'I am angry with you and your two friends, God said to one, 'because you have not spoken of me what is right, as my servant Job has'" (Job 42:7).[4]

When you are ministering to people who live with chronic illness, they are often dealing with depression, anger, fear, and a multitude of other emotions. Each individual is on his or her own journey. The life of a person is severely impacted when she is diagnosed with a chronic illness, and her roles, dreams, attitudes, and emotions easily go spinning out of control. Getting out of bed, getting dressed, and coming to church may be the biggest accomplishment she has made all week, and the last thing you want to do is to say something accusing, judgmental, ignorant, or hurtful.

We are not to presume to know why someone is suffering. Jesus' disciples asked Him "Who sinned, this man or his parents, that he was born blind?" Jesus answers "Neither this man nor his parents sinned, but this happened so that the work of God might be displayed in his life" (John 8:2,3). If even the disciples were unable to comprehend that God rarely uses illness as punishment, is it any surprise that people today still believe this?

> "I'm glad the author of Job took such care to record the rambling conversations of Job's friends: that book serves as a permanent reminder to me that I have no right to stand beside a suffering person and pronounce, 'This is the will of God,' no matter how I cloak that sentiment in pious phrases."[5]

We are to allow each person to use his gifts. Don't assume that because someone is young or looks healthy, she should be volunteering for a more physically demanding responsibility.

> "As time went on, I could no longer physically maintain the hectic schedule. I had to spend time in the hospital, so I could not fulfill the obligations I had to these groups. I was made to feel that somehow I was responsible for leaving them short-handed. When I was unable to go to church, sometimes for weeks at a time, I was basically abandoned by the friends I had there." — Bonnie

Understanding what not to say

Although people are trying to say encouraging things in this awkward situation, they often forget that the person in pain is experiencing real emotional turmoil. I call these pat answers, "God balm," and although it may feel like you are offering encouragement or telling the person to persevere, it rarely is received in the way you intended.

- "Poor health is a sign of sin. You must have some kind of hidden sin in your life.
  I didn't do anything to cause this illness. I can't cope with anymore people who only blame me. I doubt I will be returning to this church.
- "If you would just confess your sins to God, I'm sure He would heal you."
  I have confessed all that I know to confess. What happened to God's grace?
- "You are obviously not spending enough time in the Word. Haven't you read, 'Ask and you will receive'? You need to claim your healing!"
  I have asked for God's healing, and He has not given it to me. I'm also reading the Word. Maybe you don't remember how

Paul asked three times for his thorn to be removed and God said, "My grace is sufficient."

- "You must not be praying for healing right. Either you don't have enough faith or you aren't asking for the right thing. Have you used the oil like in the book of James?"

  She thinks that God can only heal me by using the oil? Maybe I don't have enough faith. Where am I going wrong, Lord? Something must be wrong with me if you are not answering my prayers.

- "All sickness is evil. It's never from God. God sent Jesus so we would not have to suffer on earth again."

  I'm doing the best I can. How can this evil have so much control over my life when I surrender it over to God every day? I'm trying so hard to do as you desire, Lord.

- "Everything works together for good."

  That's easy for you to say. You aren't the one that has to live with this. I know Romans 8:28 and I'd rather not have it quoted to me.

- "I know this isn't God's will for you."

  How do you know what God's will is for me? No one really knows.

- "Why would God let this happen to a nice person like you?"

  I'm trying to figure that out myself. You must think that there is some reason I deserve it that you don't know about.

- "He has chosen you to suffer for Him. You should be thanking Him for allowing you to bring glory to Him in this way."

  Thanking Him? Some spiritual giants may be up to this, but right now I just want my old life back. This is not how I planned on serving God.

- "I just know that you will be healed."

What if I'm not? I'm getting worse all the time. Will you blame me if I'm not healed?

- "If you pray for God to heal you, I know He will answer your prayers."

I've been praying for healing and God is not answering my prayers. Maybe I'm not praying right or I don't have enough faith or something.

- "There are so many people praying for you. God is going to answer our prayers in no time!"

What if God doesn't heal me? How do you know that God will heal me? How will you treat me if your prayers are not answered?

Can you think of some examples of God balm? What have people said to you that felt like a "token response" despite their good intentions? Most of us have heard some of these. How have you responded?

Avoid sharing cures

People who live with illness are bombarded from well-intensioned friends (and strangers) with news about vitamins, herbs, teas, pills, and alternative therapies. Church should be one place where they can be free from encountering this.

Those who live with chronic illness have usually considered alternative treatments and also consult with their physicians regarding treatment. Regarding new treatments or study findings, they may seem hesitant to get excited because they know the findings are based on preliminary studies. Many medications or treatments that you may hear about on the nightly news are years away from FDA approval and distribution. They have learned how to live with their illness and take one day at a time.

Consequences of saying the wrong thing

There are three likely consequences when a well-meaning individual says the wrong thing.

1. The person will turn away from the individual who made the comment with anger, frustration, resentment, and other negative feelings. If he is stumbling in his walk with God, he could easily refrain from attending church in the future, assuming that all Christians feel the same way.

2. Although the comment is often made by an individual, one person can easily be seen as a representative of the entire church, and it can easily affect the future attendance of the ill person. The person in pain may believe the comments that an individual makes. "When you're in pain, the problem is that it is much easier to surrender to the accusers than to resist their assault," writes Biebel.[6] Dealing with the guilt that we have somehow brought it upon ourselves can actually be *easier* to cope with than the anxiety of not having any answers.

3. On a rare occasion, comments may not affect a person or they may become numb to people's ignorance. Perhaps as their relationship with Christ has grown stronger, they can let comments slide off more easily than they once did. This is, however, a very rare occurrence. No matter how often we hear insensitivity, we rarely become used to it.

> "Those who have labored with me during these times are sympathetic mostly when I 'appear the part.' The rest of the time, although I am in constant pain trying not to complain, people avoid me when I am just going to talk about my illness. In order to have friends and fellowship, I have had to learn to pretend I am okay, which complicates things too." —Jenny

There is no indication in scripture that a person with an illness or disability is loved any less than the rest of humankind. In fact, Psaln 34:18 reassures us that "The Lord is close to the brokenhearted and saves those who are crushed in spirit." We who are brokenhearted in any way are as worthy of God's love as anyone else. The comments that people make are often out of fear, tradition, or peculiar interpretations of scripture that have been taken out of context. The mystery of human suffering and lack of fairness of who suffers bewilders us all, and we are susceptible to making thoughtless statements that can be hurtful.

So . . . what can I say?

More than any piece of advice or encouragement, what people need most is to be able to talk to someone who will just listen. They need someone who will give them a (gentle) hug. They need someone who will miss them when they are not there.

> "I was in the first year of chronic fatigue syndrome and beginning to struggle even to attend church. I began feeling, with an unfriendly group around me, why bother to attend? The church was pretty dry anyway. So I just stopped going. Only one person called to see how we were doing. I've not attended services in almost ten years and there has been no contact with members who I thought were friends. I'd been a regular there for twelve years at the time I left." — Bonnie

Communication Tips

If you don't know what to say, just tell her that. Say "I wish I knew the right thing to say, but just know that I care, and I am here if you need me." Here are some tips from my book *Beyond Casseroles: 505 Ways to Encourage a Chronically Ill Friend*.

- Focus on her needs and not on your own discomfort of not having adequate answers.

- Be physically near her, and if it is appropriate, touch her hand or give her a hug.
- Keep your words brief. Let her express what she is feeling.
- Don't pretend that you don't have struggles.
- Ask her what she would like you to pray for and assure her that you are praying for her.
- Encourage her to recall the times she has experienced God's faithfulness.
- Support her to take just one day at a time.
- Inspire her to reach out for the help she needs (friends, family, pastor).
- Ask how you can help out her family.
- Don't be artificial in trying to "cheer her up." Be genuine. Be the friend you were before trouble hit.
- Show her the love you would like other people to show you if you were in their situation.
- Acknowledge how much she hurts. Don't ignore her problem.
- Help her to realize that coping with troubles takes time. Give her time to heal. Don't rush the process.
- Send notes just to say you are thinking of her.

A friend recently shared, "I just needed to have someone be strong for me, since I couldn't be strong any more. I just wanted someone to sit beside me while I cried." This is awkward. People don't like to feel helpless. They think "There must be something more that I should be doing." There isn't. More than anything, people want to know someone cares.

Be active in determining the needs people may have

A church can take an active role in increasing their

understanding of what the needs may be of the chronically ill. One way is to conduct a survey on the needs people may have. This may be an official survey or just a needs assessment a church elder does while visiting one's home. Ask, "If a van is provided, will you be able to get to church more easily? Would you listen to church on the internet if you were too ill to attend? Do you feel you can call and ask for occasional personal assistance (especially if the illness is chronic and not acute)? Would you like the worship song lyrics in the bulletin and not just on an overhead? Are the seats comfortable or would you prefer a few rows be saved for you with cushions?"

Most people don't expect church members to line up at their doorstep with meals and babysitting for months at a time. A church can brainstorm with a group of people who have a chronic illness, such as a small group, and ask them for a wish list; then prioritize. There will be some excellent opportunities for youth groups to learn the gift of serving to meet some of the needs that arise.

How to get people to accept help

Despite the needs people may have and those that they have actually expressed, it can still be difficult to get them to accept the assistance sometimes, and you may be left wondering, "Why did I even bother to set this up if they won't accept the help?" There are a variety of people who will respond to help in different ways:

- The person who has a great deal of pride and is hesitant to ask for, or even accept help, under any circumstances may actually turn down assistance or not communicate well when it's offered.
- The person who would love assistance, but will deny it unless it's just given. For example, if you just bring

her dinner, she will graciously accept, but she would never have accepted it otherwise.

- The person who, when asked how she can be helped, will give you some specific or general ways that would be of assistance and give thanks for the offer.
- The person who has had her life turned upside down by her illness, feels totally out of control, and wants to be allowed to make all decision so that she can still maintain some control in her household.
- The person who is tired of people making assumptions about what she does and doesn't want. She'd just like to be consulted.

How do you accommodate all of these personalities? The best way is (1) Before doing anything, *ask* the person if he or she would like help; (2) Volunteer to do something specific, and confirm that it is okay.

For example:

Don't ask: "Is there anything that I can do to help out?" *She will likely answer "No, thanks. I'm fine."*

Do ask: "I noticed your lawn is getting about as tall as mine. I wouldn't mind coming over and cutting it for you Saturday afternoon. Would that be helpful?" *She'll likely answer "yes" and be grateful for your offer.*

Don't ask: "Let me know if you need me to run any errands for you this week." *One rarely asks because she doesn't know if she's interrupting.*

Do ask: "I'm going to be going to the pharmacy and grocery store Tuesday afternoon. I'd be happy to pick up whatever you need. Just make a list of anything you can think of. Would that be helpful for you?"

Have ministries that serve physical needs

The apostle James wrote, "What good is it, my brothers, if a man claims to have faith, but has no deeds? Suppose a brother or sister is without clothes and daily food. If one of you says to him, 'Go, I wish you well; keep warm and well fed,' but does nothing about his physical needs, what good is it? In the same way, faith by itself, if it not accompanied by action, is dead" James 2:14-17.

> "They need to feel God's love in the practical helps. Then they need to hear about grace. They need someone to listen to their plight and accept them in grace without running the opposite way to avoid them. They need to be needed in the church and have a part . . .for they are members and have a unique gift." — Jenny

So now you know how to go about asking, but what can you do to help out? Here are some ideas:

- A clean house
- Yardwork
- Babysitting
- Errands/transportaon

Have ministries that meet emotional needs

"Be sure you know the condition of your flocks, give careful attention to your herds." In the translation *The Message* it tells us, "Know your sheep by name." It's the little ways we let those around us know we care that mean the most. (Proverbs 27:23)

> "Postcards and offers of small favors would be wonderful. I hate the obvious stuff . . 'how are you?' questions, etc. because I usually can't answer 'fine' honestly so either I lie, or I say 'so-so' and then they want all of the details and I get all those 'poor you' looks. Less asking and more little-tiny kindnesses,

without all the explanation needed, would go a long way." — Amy

Here are a few ideas of ways to emotionally support someone in your church; some churches call this group of volunteers "HopeKeepers Helpers."

- Send notes or postcards periodically just to let her know someone is thinking of her.
- Have someone call her occasionally just to see how she is doing, but keep the conversations short.
- Have a children's Sunday school class send her a packet of pictures they have drawn for her.
- Have someone take her out to lunch occasionally.
- Have a few caring people *schedule* a visit, to bring Sunday's CD from church services or church newsletter.
- Give each person with a chronic illness an emergency contact number of someone in the church that they can call.
- Establish prayer partners for people with illness, within the church.
- Have a special visitation team that can keep in touch with people who live with chronic illness, to pray with them, see how they are doing, etc.
- Set up a buddy system so that at least one person from church calls them weekly to help them keep in touch.
- Establish a audio/media ministry to enable them to still hear the Word.
- Ask the youth group to visit and bring their enthusiasm and music to people who live with chronic illness.

"When I became ill with myasthenia gravis, everyone found out. We had just moved to this small town of a thousand people, but word traveled fast. I started to get cards and notes from people. The one message in every one of them was that they were praying for me and my family. These are people that I may never have met or may have been introduced to only once. To know that so many people cared enough to take the time to send a card to let me know that they were praying for us made me feel so strong. No matter how bad I was feeling physically, I knew that my girls and my husband would have a town to care for them. I could concentrate on myself. This has strengthened my belief in the power of prayer." —Sherrie

Consider adding a parish nurse to your staff

If your congregation has a lot of seniors this may literally be a God-send! Many retired nurses are finding this area of ministry appealing and most hospitals now offer training. Parish nurses have a variety of duties, depending on your church's needs and goals, for example, they may go to homes to monitor diabetes or high blood pressure of church members, organize health fairs and screenings, help provide walking groups, etc.

Provide helpful resources that are available to borrow

Many people with chronic illness are on a fixed-income and yet they need encouragement. Stock your church library with books on living with chronic illness, books on CDs, audio presentations, and large-print materials whenever they are available. Collect lists of local resources and national ministries for those with illness/disabilities/caregiving and put them in a binder; lists of organizations, magazines and newsletters on topics for Christian seniors, those with disabilities, caregivers, and assisted living.

Have special guest speakers

There are dozens of people who have physical disabilities

that can share their testimony during a church service or special event. Inviting them to the pulpit to share what God has done in their lives—despite physical challenges—sends a message to those who are ill that you recognize their needs, you care, and most of all, that you believe they are still worthy to be used by God.

Encourage participation in the church

One of my favorite scriptures is "He who refreshes others will himself be refreshed" (Proverbs 11:25). Remember people with illness want to serve—*not* just *be* served. For example, when someone who is ill tells you she must resign from teaching Sunday school, let her know that she is welcome to serve in other ways when she is ready. She may find she enjoys writing notes to others who have illnesses to encourage them. A man may find he can mentor another man with a chronic illness one-on-one rather than leading a Bible study.

> "The church should realize that people with chronic illness/pain are a gift to the church in the same way that anyone else is. In many ways we, too, can minister, if allowed to within our own capabilities."—Connie

There are many ways that people in pain can be of service to the church. For their well being, it could be considered vital. Each person should be encouraged to find an area of ministry where he or she can become involved and enjoy. Having the opportunity to fellowship with others will also make them feel more comfortable when they receive assistance from the church.

One person said that a church leader told her, "When you first came to our church, it seemed you would be such an asset. And now you are one of those people who is always needing something." This attitude needs to be avoided at all costs. Each person is a gift from God and as Ephesians 2:10 says, "We are God's workmanship, created in Christ Jesus to do good works, which God prepared in advance for us to do." Those who live with illness are no exception.

> "I would not want the focus from the church to be on my pain and illness, but rather I would like them to make use of the skills I have even with limitations. I would like to be informed of events at the church and be part of a prayer chain, and generally made to feel part of the congregation, whether I was there every Sunday or not." —Bonnie

Here is something important to note: people who have a chronic illness may actually *not* want to participate in a chronic illness ministry. They may want nothing to do with illness, caregiving, or congregational care ministries and that is okay. Let them know that you value wounded healers and believe that God comforts us "so that we can comfort those in *any* trouble with the comfort we ourselves have received from God" (2 Corinthians 1:4).

"One of the greatest diseases
is to be nobody to anybody."
Mother Teresa

"There may be no trumpet sound or loud applause
when we make a right decision,
just a calm sense of resolution and peace."
Gloria Gaither

"It must be a terrible thing for a man to have never to
have suffered physical pain. You say, 'I should like to be
that man.' Ah, unless you had extraordinary grace, you
would grow hard and cold; you would get to be a sort of
cast iron man, breaking other people with your touch.
No, let my heart be tender, even be soft, if it must be
softened by pain, for I would fain know how to bind up
my fellow's wound. Let my eye have a tear ready for my
brother's sorrows, even if in order to that, I should have
to shed ten thousand for my own. As escape from
suffering would be escape from the power to sympathize,
and that were to be deprecated beyond all things."
Charles Spurgeon

"Never let a problem to be solved become more
important than a person to be loved."
Barbara Johnson

CHAPTER 19
BEYOND SMALL GROUPS

Conclusion

As you have began to form a chronic illness small group ministry you have probably answered a lot of questions. People have said, "I didn't even know you had a chronic illness. You look so good!" Church leadership may have asked, "Why do we need a ministry for people with chronic illness? If God hasn't healed them, we shouldn't condone their sin by offering them a group." Perhaps when you announced your small group, you had few people sign up and others said, "There just isn't that great of a need."

The response or lack of response does not change the fact that there are large numbers of people who are hurting, and they feel invisible. They may not always be quick to sign up for a group, because they worry about becoming vulnerable. They may feel they just don't have the time. You may be excited about new Bible study materials that you have found, but no one else is. Don't despair. Remember, people don't care how much you know until they know how much you care.

Chronic illness ministry takes time. It takes time to develop friendships. It takes time for people to trust you. It takes time for them to see your motivations for leading a chronic illness small group. They want to see that you are sincere and not just another body that the church has sent over to their house to feel sorry for them and give them advice. Give it time.

If you do not live with illness or pain, I hope this book has given you the opportunity to look inside the world of the chronically ill. You may have said, "Hmm . . .I never knew that," or "I never thought of that, but it makes sense."

If you live with illness or pain, I hope that you have been able to nod in understanding, feeling as though your questions, emotions, and concerns have been acknowledged and validated. I hope that you have thought, "I'm not alone."

Yancey shares in *Where is God When it Hurts?*,

> "The French have a saying: 'To suffer passes; to have suffered never passes.' Too often we think about a ministry of helps as a one-way street in which I, the healthy person, reach out in compassion to assist the wounded. But people who have suffered are the very best equipped to help, and a person crosses the final barrier of helplessness when he or she learns to use the experience of suffering itself as a means of reaching out to others . . A wise sufferer will look not inward, but outward. There is no more effective healer than a wounded healer, and in the process the wounded healer's own scars may fade away." [1]

I hope that you can be a wounded healer. "Many Christians are superbly qualified to minister to others—and they don't even know it," writes Ray Pritchard in his book *Keep Believing*. "They are the ones who have been deeply hurt by the troubles of life—and, through it all, they have discovered that God is faithful. Those folks have an important message to share. They can say it with conviction, 'God will take care of you. I know because He took care of me.'"

*"I thank God for my handicaps, for through them,
I have found myself, my work, and my God."*
Helen Keller

*"God 'resources' us even when ministry depletes us.
God enables us when ministry baffles us.
God makes us sufficient for every situation
we encounter for Him."*
Pastors at Great Risk

*"Little ways of reaching out make all of the
difference to someone who is hurting, especially
when the illness is chronic. It's rarely the 'size' of the
task, but the simple fact that you made an effort and
remembered him or her in your thoughts."*
Lisa Copen

*"Be faithful in small things because it is in them that
your strength lies. In this life we cannot do great things.
We can only do small things with great love."*
Mother Teresa

*"Everybody can be great, because anybody can serve,
you don't have to have a college degree to serve. . .
You only need a heart full of grace.
A soul generated by love."*
Martin Luther King

CHAPTER 20
BEYOND SMALL GROUPS

Resources

Once you have decided to form a small group, you will likely start your search for materials. You may not find the abundance of resources that you would expect that are specifically Christian in nature on the topic of illness. But there are some excellent ones out there.

American Association of Disability (Interfaith)

The mission of the AAPD Interfaith Initiative is to support people with disabilities and their families as they seek spiritual and religious access, and to bring the powerful and prophetic voice of the faith community to the 21st Century disability agenda. Interfaith Initiative will urge local congregations, denominations, national faith groups, and seminaries to identify and remove barriers that prevent people with disabilities from participating in a full life of faith including worship, study, service, and leadership. As you know, these include barriers of architecture, communications, and attitude.

Contact: www.aapd.com/Interfaith/Interfaith.html or 202-521-4311

Christian Institute on Disability

Founded by Joni Eareckson Tada, this program currently has a 1-week intensive program and will soon have a Certificate in Disability Ministry available. This 32-hour certificate program is designed to give one an introductory understanding of the aspects of disability ministry. It includes an overview of disability, theology, the church and disability and introduction to bioethics. Participants will learn through lecture, group discussion, video and hands-on experience to evangelize, welcome into the church and empower those affected by disability. This program is designed for ministers, professionals, teachers, volunteers, students and anyone interested in learning more about effective disability ministry. Contact: www.joniandfriends.org or 818 -707-5664

Hospital Christian Fellowship American Association of Disability

This is an evangelical, international and interdenominational organization among those involved in the care of the sick. They provide great resources including a seminar called "Compassionate Care for the Sick and Hurting" — a free four hour seminar for active churches and healthcare groups. Includes: *Visiting the Sick: Emergencies; Difficult Questions; Spiritual Care Questions; When to Pray; Visiting Friends and Relatives; When to use Scripture; Ministering to Comatose Patients and the Terminally Ill; Guidelines for the Bereaved; Long Term Care Visitation;* etc. HCF in the USA is registered as a non-profit organization and is also registered with the Board of Registered Nurses in CA as a provider of Continuing Education. Its purpose is to teach healthcare professionals, caregivers and volunteers how to meet t he spiritual needs of their patients and fellow workers through evangelism, prayer and discipleship. This is accomplished through conferences, seminars, literature, tapes, a prayer

network, personal visits and *A New Heart* magazine.
Contact: www.hcfusa.com or 949-496-7655

Joni and Friends International Disability Center
Founded by Joni Eareckson Tada in 1979, Joni and
Friends exists to communicate the gospel and equip Christ-
honoring churches worldwide to evangelize and disciple
people affected by disability. You'll find a wealth of
information on different ministries around the world,
resources such as instructions on how to organize a disability
Sunday, Family Retreats and much more.
Contact: www.joniandfriends.org or 818 -707-5664

Mental Health Ministries
The mission of Mental Health Ministries is to provide
educational resources to help erase the stigma of mental
illness in our faith communities and help congregations
become caring congregations for persons living with a mental
illness and their families. User friendly media and print
resources that can be adapted to the unique needs of each
congregation are available on the website. Mental Health
Ministries also collaborates with faith communities, advocacy
groups, community organizations and mental health
professionals to lift up the importance of using a person's
faith and spirituality as part of the overall treatment and
recovery process.
Contact: www.MentalHealthMinistries.net

Rest Ministries, Inc.
Rest Ministries, Inc. is a ministry for people who live with
chronic illness or pain and it has small groups throughout the
United States called HopeKeepers®. They also publish and
carry a great collection of books and small group materials
that address chronic illness, depression and more from a

Christian perspective. Visit the bookstore online at
www.comfortzonebooks.com . There is a HopeKeepers
leaders message board to exchange information in the
HopeKeepers group at www.restministriessunroom.com and
sign up to receive daily devotionals by those who are ill.
Contact: www.restministries.org or 888-751-7378

Small Groups
This is a ministry of *Leadership Journal* at Christianity
Today International. They are a nonprofit
interdenominational organization whose goal is to serve the
church by changing the leaders who change the world. They
have the wonderful materials that "provide small group
leaders everything they need to inspire life-changing
community."
Contact: www.smallgroups.com

JOY Coupon
One of our greatest tools to help people put "feet on
prayers" is the book *Beyond Casseroles: 505 Ways to Encourage a
Chronically Ill Friend* published by Rest Ministries. Included in
the Appendix is a JOY Coupon (Just Offering You. . .) to give
a friend when you want to offer to help in some way.
Colorful ones are available in packs of 20 at
chronicillnessbooks.com. These are great to hand out to
everyone in your church, especially elders, congregational
care members, women's ministry groups, etc.

Reading list

Bible studies for your group
- *When Chronic Illness Enters Your Life* by Lisa Copen
- *Learning to Live with Chronic Illness* by Lisa Copen

- *Why Can't I Make People Understand* by Lisa Copen
- *The Silver Bullet: God's RX for Chronic Pain* by Jonnie Wright
- *Choices: Managing Chronic Pain* by Jonnie Wright

To further understand living with a daily chronic illness and how our choices make a difference
- *Being Well When We're Ill: Wholeness and Hope in Spite of Infirmity* by Marva J. Dawn
- *Being Sick Well: Joyful Living Despite Chronic Illness* by Jeffrey H. Boyd
- *Coping with Chronic Illness* by H. Norman Wright and Lynn Ellis

To see how the lives of those in church leadership have intersected with illness or pain
- *90 Minutes in Heaven: A True Story of Death & Life* by Don Piper, Cecil Murphey
- *Prayers and Promises When Facing a Life-Threatening Illness: 30 Short Morning and Evening Reflections* by Ed Dobson

To understanding small groups better
- *Leading Life-Changing Small Groups* by Phil Donohue
- *Simple Small Groups: A User-Friendly Guide for Small Group Leaders* by Bill Search
- *The 8 Habits of Effective Small Group Leaders* by Dave Earley
- *The Seven Deadly Sins of Small Group Ministry: A Troubleshooting Guide for Church Leaders* by Bill Donahue

To prepare for leading your group
- *Now That's a Good Question!: How to Lead Quality Bible Discussions* by Terry Powell
- *How to Lead Small Groups* by Neil McBride

- *The Pocket Guide to Burnout-Free Small Group Leadership: How to gather a core team and lead from the second chair* by Michael C. Mack
- *How to Have Great Small-Group Meetings: Dozens of Ideas You Can Use Right Now* by Neal McBride
- *How to Lead a GREAT Cell Group Meeting* by Joel Comiskey

To prepare for the tough questions you may receive regarding healing and suffering:
- *Will God Heal Me?: God's Power and Purpose in Suffering* by Ron Dunn
- *When God Weeps: Why Our Sufferings Matter to the Almighty* by Joni Eareckson Tada and Steve Estes

To find ways for your group or church to further encourage the chronically ill
- *Beyond Casseroles: 505 Ways to Encourage a Chronically Ill Friend* by Lisa Copen

To become a more effective leader and find personal encouragement
- *More Leadership Lessons of Jesus: A Timeless Model for Today's Leaders* by Bob Briner and Ray Pritchard
- *The 360 Degree Leader: Developing Your Influence from Anywhere in the Organization* by John C. Maxwell,
- *Jesus on Leadership* by C. Gene Wilkes and Calvin Miller
- *Lead Like Jesus: Lessons from the Greatest Leadership Role Model of All Time* by Ken Blanchard and Phil Hodges
- *The Power of Vision: Discover and Apply God's Vision for Your Life & Ministry* George Barna

Appendix

PREPARATION CHECKLIST

Questions to ask yourself:
- Why do I feel called to lead a group?
- Have I spent time in prayer about it?
- What fears or concerns do I have?
- Do I have the right motives for leading the group?
- Am I willing to invest my time and energy into this ministry and allow God total control, even if it means that attendance may be low sometimes?
- Have I spoken to my family or loved ones who will be affected by my decision to lead this group?
- Have I acknowledged the difference between helping and enabling and feel I can set healthy boundaries?
- Am I willing to put prayer as the first priority in my ministry?
- Would it be helpful for me to have a personal mission statement?
- What do I believe about healing and suffering? Do I feel comfortable having conversations about it?

To do:
- Purchase a small notebook and two 3-ring binders. Use 1 binder to organize your thoughts, another for all the resources you collect that you can share with members.
- Ask people around you, (friends, church members, and strangers) if they would find a small group chronic illness ministry helpful
- Prepare your testimony to share with your church when you present your group idea.
- Go through the list below of *decisions to make.*

- Organize items you will have on a resource table at your meetings.
- Start a box with group items to transport to your meeting.
- Write a press release and announcements (50 words, 200 words, etc.) about your group.
- Put together a welcome packet for new members.
- Order any items necessary for your group.
- Decide on ice breakers or other activities for your group.
- Don't forget to pray!
- Evaluate your group and what you could do to improve it.

Decisions to make:
- Will my group be Christ-based?
- What are the priorities of my group? (label 1 as most important)

Prayer—will you open and close in prayer? Will you have time for individual prayer requests? What will be your plan if individual prayer requests take a longer time than you have allotted?

_____ Worship—will there be music?

_____ Fellowship—will there be time committed to sharing about one another's concerns or praises?

_____ Bible study—there will be a lesson/book?

_____ Evangelism—will members go out into the community and share about their faith?

_____ Education and Education and Information—will your group be a place where people can bring in information or resources about individual illnesses, treatment options, alternative medicine or other educational type resources?

_____ Service—will your group serve the church or community?

_____ Social activities — will the group get together outside of the group?

_____ Other — what are some other areas of ministry you would like to see addressed in your group setting?

- Who do I know who could be a co-leader or assistant?
- Who do I know who would likely attend?
- Who will attend this group? (Does gender, illness, or age matter?)
- What is my group's Mission Statement?
- What is my group's Vision Statement? Have I used action words?
- What will make my group unique and determine its atmosphere?
- What will the lifespan of my group be? (A certain time period of continuous?)
- How frequently will the group meet?
- Will the group be open to join at any time or just during certain time periods?
- Is the group open to community members or just church members?
- Can group members bring a friend, spouse, or caregiver?
- What Bible study will my group do?
- If people need transportation, how will this be arranged?
- Determine the meeting location. It is accessible, easy to find, and comfortable?
- What is the best day of the week and time?
- How will expenses be covered?
- Have I asked group members how they would like to be contacted? Who has the option to use the internet?
- What are my group policies and guidelines? How will I inform members of them?

Ask your church leadership:

- Is there any small group training I need to do?
- Should people be asked to read and sign a mission statement who are in group leadership?
- Who in the church do I contact if I feel a situation needs emergency assistance? Who do I call in the middle of the night?
- Who do I contact if a person has financial needs, such as he needs emergency housing or money for an electric bill?
- How does the church prefer I keep them updated on how the group is functioning?
- Does the church have requirements that speakers need to meet, such as agreeing to the church's Statement of Faith?
- Would a member of pastoral staff write a letter that can be included in the welcome packet?
- How often will the group be able to have an announcement in the bulletin or have someone announce it in church?
- Does the church have a viewpoint on healing? [And do, the group leader, agree? If not, how might this impact your group leadership?]
- What expenses if the church able to assist with? (Bible studies for those who cannot afford them, photocopying, leadership materials, etc.)
- Will you review my group policies and guidelines and provide feedback?
- Do you feel the church is receptive to hearing ideas about how to increase our outreach to the chronically ill? Who would I talk to about ideas the group may have?

SAMPLE PROPOSAL FOR GROUP TO TAKE TO THE CHURCH

The purpose of the group I am proposing is:

_____

It is my hope that people will gain the following from the group

_____

I believe there is a need for this group because _____.
Statistically, a need is shown by _____. I feel called to
begin this group because _____.

The national para-church ministry that has HopeKeepers Groups is Rest
Ministries, Inc. They incorporated in 1997 and are an affiliate ministry of
Joni and Friends International Disability Center and the ministry of Joni
Eareckson Tada.

We will be meeting (____frequency____) at (____time____) I would like
to have our group meet at (____location____) . The materials we
need are listed on a separate page. The approximate cost of these items
are $_____.

My co-leader will be _____ and I have
spoken to about _____ people who would be interested in attending
the group. I would like you to review the attached pages, which include
my viewpoint on healing and other plans and logistics for this group.

EXAMPLE WELCOME LETTER FROM HOPEKEEPERS LEADER

Dear HopeKeepers® Participant,

We want to welcome you to this special group we hope will meet your spiritual and emotional needs. We hope you will feel comfortable and safe here. That this will be a place for you to share both your concerns and praises about living with chronic illness or pain. We hope that the encouragement, support and accountability that you receive in this group will lead to deep and authentic relationships. And finally, that this group will help you learn to apply the Word to your circumstances and reveal your true value in Christ.

God's Blessings,

Winny and Catharine
ALCF HopeKeepers® Leaders

EXAMPLE GUIDELINES

HopeKeepers® Group Guidelines

We're so happy you are here! It is our desire that the group be a place where you feel free to share what you are going through, a place of support and encouragement. In order to meet this goal, we ask the following of each participant:

1. We want this to be a place where people feel safe to share. Please keep what is shared in the group confidential.
2. Rather than giving each other advice, this group is about encouraging others through God's word and validating each other's experience. Here are some examples of this type of response:
   "... that sounds like a frustrating experience."
   "... I can see how that experience would cause you to feel alone."
   "Thank you for sharing. What a blessing it has been to see you rely on God's strength to get to the point you are at now."
3. Since our time together is limited, we ask that participants be sensitive to not interrupt others and to share for the specified amount of time.
4. God has called each of us here for a purpose. We are blessed by each person's participation no matter how severe or mild their pain/illness may be. Although we each will discuss the various aspects of our illness in the group, it is important that we refrain from comparing our physical limitations with each other.
5. Many people are seeking a refuge away from discussions of various treatments. If someone shares "she tried Chinese herbs and found them to be helpful," we will focus on her experience of improvement, not her method of improvement. If you find you want to discuss the treatment in more depth, we encourage you to do so after the meeting.
6. We want to respect each of the participant's medical decisions as they are shared within the group. If you have information that you believe would be helpful to someone in the group, ask them if you can mail them the information and allow them to get back to you regarding the information if and when they are ready to do so.
7. The meeting will begin at 3:00 with fellowship for the first 15 minutes, opening prayer at 3:15, and ending at about 4:45, followed by more time for fellowship.
8. Please feel free to get up and stretch or stand at any time you feel the need to. We will also plan a stretch-break during the meeting.
9. We will have a time of sharing praises and prayer requests during the last part of our meeting. We encourage everyone to participate and to keep others in the group in prayer through the month.

10. We would also like to ask that if you have the flu or a cold or think that you may be getting sick, that you not come to the group. Many people with chronic illness/ pain have auto-immune disorders that cause them to succumb to illness very easily.

Thank you.

<u>EXAMPLE HOPEKEEPERS HELPERS SIGN UP SHEET</u>

Name _____

Address _____

Phone number

Cell number

Hours/days that are best for me

Hours/days that I *cannot* volunteer _____

I would be able to contribute in the following ways: *(please check)*
- ☐ Running errands
- ☐ Making a meal
- ☐ Visiting someone in their home
- ☐ Babysitting
- ☐ Making a telephone call
- ☐ Being an emergency contact
- ☐ Yard work
- ☐ Repairs
- ☐ House cleaning
- ☐ Sending encouraging notes.
- ☐ Administrative (helping organize other volunteers)
- ☐ Other

Approx. number of hours per week I can volunteer: _____

Thank you! Someone will be contacting you.

EXAMPLE PRESS RELEASE

=======================================

For Immediate Release
Contact: YOUR NAME
             YOUR PHONE NUMBER
             CHURCH PHONE NUMBER

=======================================

Local Church Begins Chronic Illness Support Group

[Your church name], located at [your church's address] will be starting a HopeKeepers® support group/Bible study for people who live with chronic illness or pain on [date]. HopeKeepers® is a program of Rest Ministries, Inc., a San Diego-based ministry that serves the chronically ill across the country. The meetings will be held at [place] from [time to].

[your name], who lives with [your illness] decided to begin the group because [your reasons.]

Lisa Copen, founder of Rest Ministries, Inc. says, "Support and encouragement is a necessary part of learning to live successfully with a chronic illness. Support groups that are sponsored by many national health organizations can be effective; however, many people leave feeling more depressed than when they came. Oftentimes, we need to be able to share our spiritual journey and the spiritual struggles we have, a HopeKeepers is a place a person can be surrounded by others who understand both the pain, and the emotions that accompany it."

Attendance is free, but seating is limited, so please call [your phone number] to reserve a seat.

[quote from you or your pastor, etc.]

Find out more at the church web site at: [church web site address]

* * *

=======================================

EXAMPLE HOPEKEEPERS PRAYER

Creator, Almighty One,
May today there be peace within each of us.

May we trust that You have called us to be here and that this is where we are meant to be?

May You help us to remember the infinite possibilities that are born of faith, not only in You, but in ourselves and those around us.

May we, even in our brokenness, use the gifts that You have given us, and pass on the hope and love that we find in Your presence.

May You teach us to be content with ourselves just the way we are and to recognize You in everyone we meet and in all creation.

Lord, let the wisdom and grace You provide settle into our bones, and allow our souls the freedom to sing, dance, praise, hope and love even when our bodies ache. Grant us the grace and understanding to share our gifts with others in whatever way possible so that Your presence on earth is known.

We ask this in Your name,
Amen

By: Rev. Karen M Clarke, MA HopeKeepers Leader
First-Plymouth Congregational Church

EXAMPLE TOPICS

August: The Question of Why

Do you often wonder why? Why do I live in pain? Why am I so often sick and others are well? Why am I the person with the chronic illness? This meeting will discuss this difficult question and look at some new perspectives on the question of "why?"

September: Coping

What techniques and skills are helpful when coping with chronic illness? How might I best learn to live with my pain or chronic disease? This meeting will discuss techniques for coping, exercises to develop new skills and members will share what works best for them.

October: Dealing with Pain and Suffering

How does a person live with and move through chronic pain and suffering? What roles do pain and suffering play in our lives? This meeting will consider different perspectives on life with chronic pain and suffering.

November: Relationships

How does life with chronic illness impact our relationships with ourselves and others? How does a person reach out for support when friends seem to have turned away? There is no doubt that life with chronic illness and pain changes the ways we relate. These changes and ways of coping with them will be the topic for this meeting.

December: Humor and Joy

Is humor truly the best remedy? What role can humor and joy play in improving the quality of life for those with chronic illness? Join us for some great discussion and a few healing laughs.

By: Rev. Karen M Clarke, MA HopeKeepers Leader
First-Plymouth Congregational Church

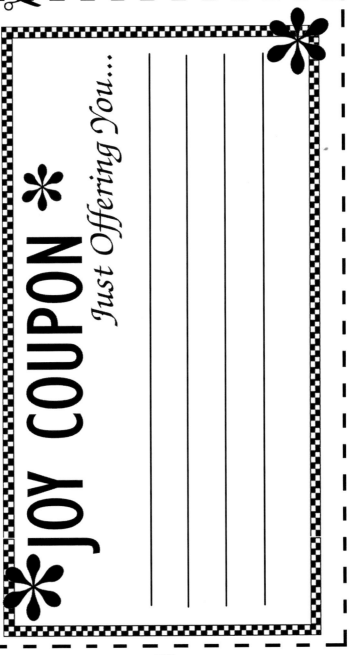

JOY COUPON

Just Offering You....

Notes

INTRODUCTION ....

[1] Ogden, Greg and Daniel Meyer. *Leadership Essentials: Shaping Vision, Multiplying Influence, Defining Character* (Downers Grove: IVP Connect 2007), 88.

[2] Eareckson Tada, Joni and Steven Estes. *When God Weeps: Why Our Sufferings Matter to the Almighty* (Grand Rapids: Zondervan, 2000), 101.

[3] Yancey, Philip. *Disappointment with God: Three Questions No One Asks Aloud* (Grand Rapids: Zondervan, 2002), 264.

[4] Job 42:1,2,10,12,16, 17

[5] Egli, Jim. "A Small-Group Leader's Most Important Job" Small Groups. Feb. 15, 2010, www.smallgroups.com/articles/2010/sgleadersmostimportantjob.html

CHAPTER 1 ....

[1] Donogue, Paul. Personal Phone Conversation. 2006. Author of *Sick and Tired of Feeling Sick and Tired: Living with Invisible Chronic Illness,* (New York City: W. W. Norton, 1994).

[2] Anderson, Gerard, Robert Herbert, Timothy Zeffiro, and Nikia Johnson, comps. "Chronic Conditions: Making the Case for Ongoing Care" (Baltimore: John Hopkins University, Partnership for Solutions, Sept 2004) Website: http://tinyurl.com/y8a8pal. Page 9.

[3] Ibid 9

[4] "Bureau of the Census, Statistical Brief: Americans With Disabilities." (1994). U.S. Department of Commerce. Publication SB/94-1. "Bureau of the Census, Census Brief: Disabilities Affect One-Fifth of All Americans."(1997) U.S. Department of Commerce. Publication CENBR/97-5.

[5] Crabb, Larry, *Inside Out,* (Colorado Springs: NavPress, 2007), 234.

CHAPTER 2 ....

[1] National Health Interview Survey

[2] Rifkin, A. "Depression in Physically Ill Patients," *Postgraduate Medicine* Sep 1;92(3):147-9, 153-4.

[3] Mackenzie TB, Popkin MK: "Suicide in the Medical Patient," *Intl J Psych in Med* 17:3-22, 1987

[4] Michalon M: La psychiatrie de consultation-liaison: une etude prospective en milieu hospitalier general. *Can J Psychiatry* (In French) 38:168-174,1993

[5] Pressman P., Lyons J.S., Larson D.B., Strain, J.J. "Religious belief, depression, and ambulation status in elderly women with broken hips." *American Journal of Psychiatry* 1990; 147(6): 758-760.

[6] Yi, Michael S. and Maria T. Britto, Susan N. Sherman, M. Susan Moyer, Sian Cotton, Uma R. Kotagal, Deborah Canfield, Frank W. Putnam, Steven Carlton-Ford, Joel Tsevat "Health Values in Adolescents with or without Inflammatory Bowel Disease" 25 November 2008, *The Journal of Pediatrics*, April 2009. Vol. 154, Issue 4, Pages 527-534.

[7] Curlin FA, et al, "Physicians' Observations and Interpretations of the Influence of Religion and Spirituality on Health" *Archives of Internal Medicine,* 2007; 167:649-654.

[8] Kendler, K.S., Gardner, C. O., and Prescott, C.A. "Religion, Psychopathology, and Substance Use and Abuse: A Multimeasure, Genetic-Epidemiologic Study," *American Journal of Psychiatry* 1997; 154: 322-329. Koenig, Harold G., David B. Larson and Andres J. Weaver, "Research on Religion and Serious Mental Illness," in *Spirituality and Religion in Recovery from Mental Illness*, ed., Roger Fallott. *New Directions for Mental Health Services* 1998; (80).

[9] Yancey, Philip. *Where Is God When It Hurts?* (Grand Rapids: Zondervan, 2002), 10.

[10] Betenbaugh, as quoted in *So You Want to Start a Chronic Illness Pain Ministry,* Copen, Lisa (San Diego: Rest Ministries Publishers, 2002).

[11] George M. Adams

CHAPTER 3 ....

[1] LeMaistre, JoAnn, Ph.D. *After the Diagnosis: From Crisis to Personal Renewal for Patients With Chronic Illness,* (Berkeley: Ulysses Press, 1995). 5.

[2] Barna, George. "Church Priorities for 2005 Vary Considerably" (Ventura: The Barna Group, 2005). www.barna.org

[3] Whyte, 1995, Turner, 1984 in "Religion and Disability Studies: Thoughts on Status and Future of an Emerging Dialogue." Eieslane, Nancy, L. Ph.D., Assistant Professor, Sociology of Religion, Candler School of Theology, Emory University, Atlanta, GA. in *Disability Studies Quarterly*, Summer 1995, Volume 15, No. 3.

[4] Eieslane, Nancy, L. Ph.D. "Religion and Disability Studies: Thoughts on Status and Future of an Emerging Dialogue." Assistant Professor, Sociology of Religion, Candler School of Theology, Emory University, Atlanta, GA. in *Disability Studies Quarterly*, Summer 1995, Volume 15, No. 3. Assistant Professor, Sociology of Religion, Candler School of Theology, Emory University, Atlanta, GA.

[5] Ibid

[6] Ibid

[7] Blair and Blair. "Pastoral Counselors/Religious Professionals and People with Disabilities" in *Disability Studies Quarterly,* Summer 1995, Volume 15, No. 3.

[8] Koenig, Harold George. *Is Religion Good for Your Health?: The Effects of Religion on Physical and Mental Health* (New York City: Routledge , 1997) 29.

[9] Duke University's Center for the Study of Religion, Spirituality and Health at www.spiritualityandhealth.duke.edu/about/hkoenig/

[10] Koenig, Harold George. *Is Religion Good for Your Health?: The Effects of Religion on Physical and Mental Health,* (New York City: Routledge , 1997) 30.

[11] Larson, David, M.D. "Religion and Spirituality in Medicine: Research and Education" *The Journal of the American Medical Association*, September 3, 1997.

[12] Eareckson Tada, Joni and Steve Miller. *Through the Roof: A Manual to Assist Churches in Developing an Effective Disability Ministry and Outreach*, (Agoura Hills: Joni and Friends International Disability Center, 2006),28. Reprinted with permission Feb. 2010 by Joni and Friends. The original survey is on file at Joni and Friends.

CHAPTER 4 ....

[1] Ryan, Dale S. "Customizing Personal Ministry" in *Building Your Church Through Counsel and Care: 30 Strategies to Transform Your Ministry* Marshall Shelley. (Ada; Bethany House Publishers, 1997) 168.

[2] Saddleback Church web site. Reference: www.saddlebackfamily.com/home/careprayerhelp/support_groups/
[3] www.lifeshealingchoices.com
[4] Celebrate Recovery web site posting, January 16, 2009; http://www.celebraterecovery.com/?p=215
[5] Cordeiro, Wayne. *Leading on Empty: Refilling Your Tank and Renewing Your Passion,* (Ada; Bethany House Publishers, 2010) 97.
[6] Morgan, Tony and Tim Stevens. *Simply Strategic Volunteers: Empowering People For Ministry,* (Loveland: Group Publishing, 2005) 148.

CHAPTER 5 ....
[1] Jacinto, Zanina. *And He Will Lift You Up: A Message of Hope in Disability, Depression, or Fear,* (2010) 28.
[2] Blackaby, Henry. *Experiencing God: Knowing and Doing the Will of God,* (Nashville: B&H Publishing, 2008) 64.
[3] Wilkes, C. Gene and Calvin Miller, *Jesus on Leadership, Discovering the Secrets if Servant Leadership from the Life of Christ,* (Carol Stream: Tyndale, 1998) 145.
[4] Copen, Lisa. "And He Will Give You Rest." In Eng, Elaine Leong Eng, MD and David B. Biebel, DMin. *The Transforming Power of Story* (Healthy Life Press, 2010)
[5] Wilkes, C. Gene and Calvin Miller, *Jesus on Leadership, Discovering the Secrets if Servant Leadership from the Life of Christ,* (Carol Stream: Tyndale, 1998) 77.
[6] Cloud, Henry and John Townsend. *Boundaries: When to Say Yes, How to Say No to Take Control of Your Life,* (Grand Rapids: Zondervan, 1992) 29.
[7] Mack, Michael C. *The Pocket Guide to Burnout-Free Small Group Leadership: How to Gather a Core Team and Lead from the Second Chair,* (Houston: Touch Outreach Ministries, 2009)
[8] Cordeiro, Wayne. *Leading on Empty: Refilling Your Tank and Renewing Your Passion,* (Ada; Bethany House Publishers, 2010) 74.
[9] Groom, Nancy. *From Bondage to Bonding: Escaping Codependency, Embracing Biblical Love,* (Colorado Springs: Navpress, 1991)

CHAPTER 6 ....

[1] Sikora, Pat. "What to Look for in a Co-Leader" February 7, 2007, whydidntyouwarnme.com/2007/02/20/what-to-look-for-in-a-co-leader. Author of *Why Didn't You Warn Me? How to Deal with Challenging Small Group Leaders.*

[2] Wilkes, C. Gene and Calvin Miller, *Jesus on Leadership, Discovering the Secrets if Servant Leadership from the Life of Christ,* (Carol Stream: Tyndale, 1998) 18.

[3] Barna, George. *The Power of Vision: Discover and Apply God's Vision for Your Life & Ministry,* (Ventura: Regal, 2009) 35.

[4] Ibid, 44.

[5] Rest Ministries, Inc. restministries.com/about/

[6] Joni and Friends, www.joniandfriends.org/about_us.php

[7] Dave Dravecky's Outreach of Hope Ministry, www.endurance.org/index.cfm/pageID/177/

[8] Maxwell, John. C., *Leadership Promises for Every Day: A Daily Devotional* (Nashville: Thomas Nelson, 2007) 25.

[9] Maxwell, John C. *The 21 Indispensable Qualities of a Leader: Becoming the Person Others Will Want to Follow* (Nashville: Thomas Nelson, 2007) 150.

[10] Ibid, 151.

[11] Used with permission by the Ohio Literacy Resource Center

[12] Logaan, Robert E. and Larry Short. *Mobilizing for Compassion: Moving People into Ministry,* (Grand Rapids: Fleming H Revell Co, 1994)

CHAPTER 7 ....

[1] Search, Bill. *Simple Small Groups: A User-Friendly Guide for Small Group Leader,* (Grand Rapids: Baker Books, 2008) 28.

[2] Ibid, 35.

CHAPTER 8 ....

[1] Eareckson Tada, Joni. *Pearls of Great Price: 366 Daily Devotional Readings,* (Grand Rapids: Zondervan, 2006) p. July 3

CHAPTER 9 ....

[1] The web site of Town and Cloudsend, article "Effective Small Groups and the Christian Counselor"
www.cloudtownsend.com/library/articles/EffectiveSmallGroups.php

[2] Smith, Sybil D. *Parish Nursing: A Handbook for the New Millen,* (New York City: Routledge, 2003) 6.

[3] Koenig, Harold G. "Foreward" p. xiv. Smith, Sybil D. *Parish Nursing: A Handbook for the New Millennium,* (New York City: Routledge, 2003)

[4] Christian, Randy "Support Groups May be Worth the Trouble" in *Building Your Church Through Counsel and Care: 30 Strategies to Transform Your Ministry* Marshall Shelley, (Ada; Bethany House Publishers, 1997) 139.

[5] Wilkes, C. Gene and Calvin Miller, *Jesus on Leadership, Discovering the Secrets of Servant Leadership from the Life of Christ,* (Carol Stream: Tyndale, 1998) 99.

[6] Donahue, Phil. *Leading Life-Changing Small Groups,* (Grand Rapids: Zondervan, 2002) 194.

CHAPTER 10 ....

[1] Rotholz, James M. *Chronic Fatigue Syndrome, Christianity, and Culture,* (Binghampton: Haworth Press, 2002.) 23.

[2] Anderson, Gerard, Robert Herbert, Timothy Zeffiro, and Nikia Johnson, comps. "Chronic Conditions: Making the Case for Ongoing Care" (Baltimore: John Hopkins University, Partnership for Solutions, Sept 2004) Website: http://tinyurl.com/y8a8pal

[3] Roberts, J.A.; Brown, D.; Elkins, T and Larson, D.B. (1997). "Factors Influencing Views of Patients with Gynecological Cancer About End-of-Life Decisions." *American Journal of Obstetrics and Gynecology* 176 (1): 166-172. June 11, 1997

[4] June 1996. Bradley DE. (1995). Religious involvement and social resources: Evidence from the data set "Americans' Changing Lives." Journal for the Scientific Study of Religion 34(2):259-267). Harris, R.C., et. al. (1995). "The Role of Religion in Heart Transplant Recipients' Long-Term Health and Well-Being." *Journal of Religion and Health* 34(1):17-32. (Feb 97).

[5] Kendler, K.S., Gardner, C. O., and Prescott, C.A. "Religion, Psychopathology, and Substance Use and Abuse: A Multimeasure, Genetic-Epidemiologic Study," American Journal of Psychiatry 1997; 154: 322-329. Koenig, Harold G., Larson, David B., and Weaver, Andrew J. "Research on Religion and Serious Mental Illness," in *Spirituality and*

Religion in Recovery from Mental Illness, ed., Roger Fallott. New Directions for Mental Health Services 1998; (80).: "Suicide in the medical patient.". Intl J Psych in Med 17:3-22, 1987.

6 Anderson, Gerard, Robert Herbert, Timothy Zeffiro, and Nikia Johnson, comps. "Chronic Conditions: Making the Case for Ongoing Care" (Baltimore: John Hopkins University, Partnership for Solutions, Sept 2004) Website: http://tinyurl.com/y8a8pal., American Cancer Society, National Health Interview Survey, Rifkin, A. "Depression in Physically Ill Patients," Postgraduate Medicine (9-92) 147-154. Pressman P., Lyons J.S., Larson D.B., Strain, J.J. "Religious belief, depression, and ambulation status in elderly women with broken hips." *American Journal of Psychiatry* 1990; 147(6): 758-760. Mackenzie TB, Popkin MK

7 The National Organization on Disability. *Religious Participation: Facts and Statistics.* www.nod.org/religion/index.cfm

8 Ibid

9 Ibid

10 Susan Reynolds Whyte. "Disability Between Discourse and Experience" in *Disability Studies Quarterly,* Summer 1995, Volume 15, No. 3.

11 Blair and Blair. "Pastoral Counselors/Religious Professionals and People with Disabilities" in *Disability Studies Quarterly,* Summer 1995, Volume 15, No. 3.

12 Blair and Blair. "Pastoral Counselors/Religious Professionals and People with Disabilities" in *Disability Studies Quarterly,* Summer 1995, Volume 15, No. 3.

13 Edwards, Laurie. *Life Disrupted: Getting Real About Chronic Illness in Your Twenties and Thirties,* (New York City: Walker & Company, 2008) 17.

14 Rotholz, James M. *Chronic Fatigue Syndrome, Christianity, and Culture,* (Binghampton: Haworth Press, 2002.) 24.

CHAPTER 11 ....

1 Blanchard, Ken and Phil Hodges. *Lead Like Jesus: Lessons from the Greatest Leadership Role Model of All Time,* (Nashville: Thomas Nelson, 2005) 83.

2 Worksheet from Rick Warren, www.exploregrace.com/Resources/YourStory.pdf

[3] Blackaby, Henry. *Experiencing God: Knowing and Doing the Will of God*, (Nashville: B&H Publishing, 2008) 77.

CHAPTER 12 ....
[1] Egli, Jim. "A Small-Group Leader's Most Important Job" Feb. 15, 2010, smallgroups.com study, www.smallgroups.com/articles/2010/sgleadersmostimportantjob.html
[2] Cordeiro, Wayne. *Leading on Empty: Refilling Your Tank and Renewing Your Passion,* (Ada; Bethany House Publishers, 2010) 31.

CHAPTER 13 ....
[1] Friesen, James G. and E. James Wilder, Anne M. Bierling, and Rick Koepcke *The Life Model: Living from the Heart Jesus Gave You, The Essentials of Christian Living,* Revised 2000-R, (Shepherd's House, 2004)
[2] Mack, Michael C. *The Pocket Guide to Burnout-Free Small Group Leadership: How to Gather a Core Team and Lead from the Second Chair,* (Houston: Touch Outreach Ministries, 2009)
CHAPTER 14 ....
[1]Original source: Joel Comiskey, (Houston: TOUCH Outreach Ministries, 2001) 34.
[2] Warren, Rick. *The Purpose-Driven Life: What on Earth am I Here For?,* (Grand Rapids: Zondervan, 2002) 33.

CHAPTER 15 ....
[1] Donahue, Phil. *Leading Life-Changing Small Groups*, (Grand Rapids: Zondervan, 2002) 84.
[2] McBride, Neal. *How to Lead Small Groups*, (Colorado Springs: NavPress, 1990) 96.
[3] Wilkes, C. Gene and Calvin Miller, *Jesus on Leadership, Discovering the Secrets if Servant Leadership from the Life of Christ,* (Carol Stream: Tyndale, 1998) 162.
[4] Earley, Dave. *The 8 Habits of Effective Small Group Leaders,* (Houston: Touch Outreach Ministries, 2009) 27.

CHAPTER 16 ....
[1] Beibel, David. *If God is so Good, Why do I Hurt So Bad?,* (New Spire Publishing, 1997)

2 Hurst, Jane. "Disability from the Point of View of Religion and Spirituality" in *Disability Studies Quarterly*, Summer 1995, Volume 15, No. 3.

3 Biebel, David. *How to Help a Heartbroken Friend: What to Do and What to Say When a Friend Is Going Through Tough Times*, (Pasadena: Hope Publishing House, 2004) 51.

4 Dobson, Edward G., *Prayers and Promises When Facing a Life-Threatening Illness: 30 Short Morning and Evening Reflections*, (Grand Rapids: Zondervan, 2007) 63.

5 Hurst, Jane. "Disability from the Point of View of Religion and Spirituality" in *Disability Studies Quarterly*, Summer 1995, Volume 15, No. 3.

6 Tada, Joni Eareckson. Response to "If you had enough faith you could be healed. . . " The web site of Joni and Friends, FAQ page: www.joniandfriends.org/faq.php

7 Hansel, Tim. *You Gotta Keep Dancin'*, (Colorado Springs: Cook Communications, 1998) 123

8 Dunn, Ron. *Will God Heal Me?: God's Power and Purpose in Suffering*, (Colorado Springs: Cook Communications, 2007) 192

CHAPTER 17 ....

1 Copen, Lisa. *Why Can't I Make People Understand? Discovering the Validation Those with Chronic Illness Seek and Why*, (San Diego: Rest Ministries Publishers, 2004) 119.

2 Amundsen, Darrell W. *The Anguish and Agonies of Charles Spurgeon*, (Chapel Library) 25.

3 Tada, Joni Eareckson. Response to "Why does God allow suffering? " The web site of Joni and Friends, FAQ page: www.joniandfriends.org/faq.php

4 Tada, Joni Eareckson and Steven Estes, *When God Weeps: Why Our Sufferings Matter to the Almighty*, (Grand Rapids: Zondervan, 2000), 64.

5 "How to Keep From Getting Hurt in a Church," Dale Robbins, 1995, a publication of Victorious Publications, Grass Valley, CA 95949, www.victorious.org/howhurt.htm

6 Yancey, Philip. *Where Is God When It Hurts?*, (Grand Rapids: Zondervan, 2002) 137,138.

7 Ibid.

[8] Biebel, David. *If God is So Good, Why Do I Hurt So Bad?* (Grand Rapids: Fleming H. Revell, 1995)

CHAPTER 18 ....

[1] Blair and Blair. "Pastoral Counselors/Religious Professionals and People with Disabilities" in *Disability Studies Quarterly*, Summer 1995, Volume 15, No. 3.

[2] "How to Keep From Getting Hurt in a Church," Dale Robbins, 1995, a publication of Victorious Publications, Grass Valley, CA 95949, www.victorious.org/howhurt.htm

[3] Yancey, Philip. *Where Is God When It Hurts?*, (Grand Rapids: Zondervan, 2002) 193.

[4] Ibid, 89.

[5] Ibid, 96.

[6] Biebel, David. *If God is So Good, Why Do I Hurt So Bad?*, (Grand Rapids: Fleming H. Revell, 1995)

CHAPTER 19 ....

[1] Yancey, Philip. *Where Is God When It Hurts?*, (Grand Rapids: Zondervan, 2002) 193.

MORE BOOKS FROM REST MINISTRIES

Order at illnessbooks.com or 858-486-4685. The web site has complete descriptions and current prices.

Mosaic Moments: Devotionals for the Chronically Ill
212 pages

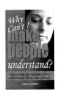

Why Can't I Make People Understand?
Discovering the Validation those with Chronic Illness
Seek and Why
138 pages

Bible Studies:
(1) When Chronic Illness Enters Your Life (2) Learning to Live with Chronic Illness, 5 lessons each for individuals or groups

Beyond Casseroles: 505 Ways to Encourage
a Chronically Ill Friend
105 pages

ABOUT REST MINISTRIES

Rest Ministries, Inc. is a non-profit Christian organization that exists to serve people who live with chronic illness or pain, and their families, by providing spiritual, emotional, relational, and practical support through a variety of resources, including HopeKeepers® small group Bible studies, daily devotionals online and a social network to connect with other people.

We also seek to bring an awareness and a change in action throughout churches in the U.S., in regard to how people who live with chronic illness or pain are served, and teach churches effective ministry tools in ministering to this population. restministries.com

NATIONAL INVISIBLE CHRONIC ILLNESS AWARENESS WEEK

National Invisible Chronic Illness Awareness Week, held annually in September, is a designated time worldwide in which people who live with chronic illness, those who love them, and organizations are encouraged to educate the general public, churches, health care professionals, and government officials about the effects of living with a disease that is not visually apparent. For more information visit .invisibleillnessweek.com or contact Rest Ministries, the sponsor of this week at 858-486-4685.